My
Google®
Chromebook

FOURTH EDITION

Michael Miller

My Google® Chromebook, Fourth Edition

Copyright © 2020 by Pearson Education, Inc.

ISBN-13: 978-0-13-591182-2
ISBN-10: 0-13-591182-6

Library of Congress Control Number: 2019908197

1 2019

Trademarks

Warning and Disclaimer

Special Sales

For information about buying this title in bulk quantities, or for special sales opportunities (which may include electronic versions; custom cover designs; and content particular to your business, training goals, marketing focus, or branding interests), please contact our corporate sales department at corpsales@pearsoned.com or (800) 382-3419.

For government sales inquiries, please contact governmentsales@pearsoned.com.

For questions about sales outside the U.S., please contact intlcs@pearson.com.

Editor-in-Chief
Brett Bartow

Executive Editor
Laura Norman

Associate Editor
Chhavi Vig

Marketing
Stephane Nakib

Editorial Services
The Wordsmithery LLC

Managing Editor
Sandra Schroeder

Project Editor
Mandie Frank

Copy Editor
Charlotte Kughen

Indexer
Cheryl Lenser

Proofreader
Sarah Kearns

Technical Editor
Karen Weinstein

Editorial Assistant
Cindy Teeters

Cover Designer
Chuti Prasertsith

Compositor
Bronkella Publishing

Graphics
T J Graham Art

Contents at a Glance

Table of Contents

CV 07.17.2019 1612

4 Using Chrome OS and the Chrome Desktop   39

8 **Configuring and Personalizing Chrome OS**   **87**

9 **Managing Files and Using External Storage**   **101**

Credits

About the Author

Michael Miller is a prolific and popular writer of more than 200 nonfiction books, known for his ability to explain complex topics to everyday readers. He writes about a variety of topics, including technology, business, and music. His best-selling books for Que include *Computer Basics: Absolute Beginner's Guide*, *My Facebook for Seniors*, *My Social Media for Seniors*, *My TV for Seniors,* and *My Windows 10 Computer for Seniors*. Worldwide, his books have sold more than 1.5 million copies.

Find out more at the author's website: www.millerwriter.com

Follow the author on Twitter: @molehillgroup

Dedication

To my wonderful grandkids Alethia, Collin, Hayley, Jackson, Jamie, Judah, and Lael.

Acknowledgments

Thanks to all the folks at Que who helped turned this manuscript into a book, including Laura Norman, Charlotte Kughen, Chhavi Vig, Mandie Frank, and technical editor Karen Weinstein.

We Want to Hear from You!

As the reader of this book, *you* are our most important critic and commentator. We value your opinion and want to know what we're doing right, what we could do better, what areas you'd like to see us publish in, and any other words of wisdom you're willing to pass our way.

We welcome your comments. You can email or write to let us know what you did or didn't like about this book—as well as what we can do to make our books better.

Please note that we cannot help you with technical problems related to the topic of this book.

When you write, please be sure to include this book's title and author as well as your name and email address. We will carefully review your comments and share them with the author and editors who worked on the book.

Email: community@informit.com

Reader Services

Register your copy of *My Google Chromebook* at quepublishing.com for convenient access to downloads, updates, and corrections as they become available. To start the registration process, go to quepublishing.com/register and log in or create an account*. Enter the product ISBN, 9780135911822, and click Submit. Once the process is complete, you will find any available bonus content under Registered Products.

*Be sure to check the box that you would like to hear from us in order to receive exclusive discounts on future editions of this product.

Understanding Chrome OS, Chromebooks, and Cloud Computing

A Chromebook is a popular type of notebook computer that's not a Mac and not a Windows PC. Instead, Chromebooks run Google's Chrome operating system—Chrome OS—a newer type of web-based operating system.

Chromebooks come in a variety of types and sizes, but all are light-weight and have very long battery life. They don't have much in the way of internal storage, but they don't need it; all of your files are stored online, in web-based storage.

All you need to run your Chromebook and access your files is an Internet connection. In fact, you can access your files from any-where, even from other Chromebooks, because they're not stored locally. It's all about what's called *cloud computing*, which uses appli-cations and data files stored in the "cloud" of the Internet, not on any individual personal computer.

Because of its web-based nature, using a Chromebook and the Chrome OS is quite a bit different from using a traditional notebook PC and either Microsoft Windows or the Mac OS. To get the most use out of your new Chromebook, you need to become familiar with how cloud computing works—as well as all the ins and outs of your new Chromebook.

What Is a Chromebook?

Put simply, a Chromebook is a notebook computer that runs the Google Chrome OS. Whereas most notebooks run a version of the Microsoft Windows or Mac OS operating systems, Chromebooks instead run Google's web-based operating system (hence the name Chromebook—a notebook running Google Chrome OS).

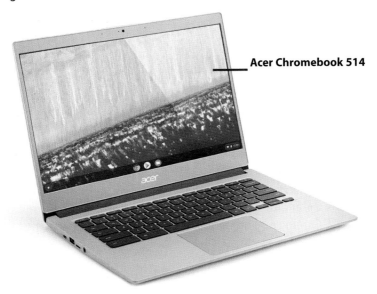

Acer Chromebook 514

Most Chromebooks are smaller and lighter than traditional notebook PCs. Because most Chromebooks don't contain a hard disk or CD/DVD drive, that space and weight is removed from the equation. Most Chromebooks have 12"–15" (or so) diagonal screens, are very thin, and weigh less than three pounds.

Chromebox

Chromebooks are portable computers. If you want a desktop computer that runs the Chrome OS, look for what is called a *Chromebox*. Acer, ASUS, CTL, and other manufacturers make Chromebox models that sell for about $150 and up.

If there's no hard drive inside, how does a Chromebook store your data? The answer is *solid state storage*, the same kind you find on USB flash drives and the memory cards you use with your digital camera. Most current Chromebooks come with 16GB to 64GB of internal solid state storage—considerably less than what you find on a traditional notebook's hard drive, but all that Chrome OS needs to run. As for storing your data, that's what the Web is for; a Chromebook needs only minimal local storage.

In terms of processing power, today's Chromebooks use one of several dual- or quad-core processors from AMD, Intel, or MediaTek. They have more than enough power to run all the web-based apps you'll be using.

This combination of small screen, minimal solid state storage, and efficient processor means that a Chromebook has an impressive battery life, 8 hours on a charge, minimum. Chromebooks are also virtually instant on; they boot up in less than 10 seconds and resume instantly from sleep mode. It's a much different—and much more efficient—computing experience than what you're probably used to.

In essence, then, a Chromebook is a computer that is built and optimized for the Web, using Chrome OS. This provides a faster, simplified, and more secure computing environment than with traditional Windows or Mac computers.

Chromebooks Online
Learn more about Chromebooks and Google Chrome OS online at www.google.com/chromebook/.

What Is Google Chrome OS?

Google's Chrome OS is the world's first operating system for the new era of cloud computing. It's a web-based operating system, in that it relies on a variety of web-based services and applications to work; it doesn't run traditional desktop applications. It's designed to be used on smallish computers that are wirelessly connected to the Internet.

Because it runs over the Web, Chrome OS is a "lightweight" operating system, in that it doesn't have a large footprint in terms of file size or memory or processing requirements. It can fit quite easily within the limited internal storage space of a small Chromebook computer, and it's automatically updated whenever the computer is connected to the Internet. It's also relatively fast and efficient, which results in short startup times and sprightly operation.

Chrome and Linux

Chrome is an open source operating system, which means that it can be freely distributed without paying expensive licensing costs. It's based on a version of Linux, another operating system that itself is based on the established UNIX operating system. The Chrome OS interface runs on top of the underlying Linux kernel.

The Chrome OS running on Chromebooks today isn't what users saw on the initial Chromebooks that shipped way back in 2011. That first iteration of Chrome OS closely resembled Google's Chrome web browser. There was no traditional desktop, as found in Microsoft Windows or Apple's Mac OS, and applications were launched in individual tabs within the Chrome browser. Using this early version of Chrome was more like browsing the Web than it was navigating a complex operating system, such as Windows.

People didn't like that browser-based interface, so Google changed it. The current version of Chrome OS features the same sort of start menu and desktop you find in Windows or the Mac OS. Applications open in their own windows on the desktop, and you can easily switch from one open window to another. It's very similar to using Microsoft Windows or the Mac OS; the big difference is that most of what you launch is housed on the Web, not locally.

The Chrome OS desktop

That's right, Chrome OS does not and cannot run traditional software programs; everything it runs must be a web-based application. This means that you can't use traditional software programs such as Microsoft Office or Adobe Photoshop, just web-based apps. (Although many companies—including Microsoft and Adobe—offer web-based versions of their traditional software programs.)

In addition, Chromebooks and Chrome OS can run apps developed for Google's Android mobile operating system. So the same apps you run on your Android phone are available to run on your Chromebook—and available for downloading from the Google Play Store.

What Is Cloud Computing?

The ability to run apps from the Web takes advantage of a technology called *cloud computing*, which represents a major shift in how we run computer applications and store data. With cloud computing, instead of applications and data being hosted on an individual desktop computer, everything is hosted in the "cloud"—a nebulous assemblage of computers and servers accessed via the Internet. Cloud computing lets you access your applications and documents from anywhere in the world, freeing you from the confines of the desktop and facilitating wholesale group collaboration.

Cloud computing connects various types of devices to a central "cloud" where applications and documents reside.

How Traditional Desktop Computing Works

Traditional desktop computing is all about the sovereignty of the individual computer. Although individual computers can be networked together, all the computer power resides on the desktop; each personal computer has its own massive amounts of memory and hard disk storage.

This storage is put to good use, to store all your programs and data. You have to install on your computer a copy of each software program you use. These programs are run from your computer's hard drive, and the documents you create are stored on the same computer and hard drive. Programs and documents are specific to individual machines.

In other words, desktop computing is computer-centric.

How Cloud Computing Works

In contrast, cloud computing doesn't depend on individual computers much at all. With cloud computing, the applications you run and the documents you create aren't stored on your personal computer; they're stored on servers you access via the Internet. If your computer crashes, the application is still available for others to use—or for you to run from another computer.

It's the same thing with the documents you create, but even more so. Because the documents are stored in the "cloud," anyone with permission not only can access the documents but can also edit and collaborate on those documents in real time.

Unlike traditional computing, then, this cloud computing model isn't computer-centric; it's user- or document-centric. Which computer you use to access a document simply isn't important; instead, the focus is on your apps and data, which you can access from anywhere, on any device—such as a Chromebook or Chromebox computer.

>>>Go Further

DEFINING THE CLOUD

Key to the definition of cloud computing is the "cloud" itself. Put simply, the cloud is a grid of interconnected computers. These computers can be personal computers or network servers; they can be public or private.

For example, Google hosts a cloud that consists of both smallish PCs and larger servers. Google's cloud is a private one (that is, Google owns it) that is publicly accessible (by Google's users).

This cloud of computers extends beyond a single company or enterprise. The applications and data served by the cloud are available to a broad group of users, cross-enterprise and cross-platform. Access is via the Internet; any authorized user can access these docs and apps from any computer over any Internet connection. And, to the user, the technology and infrastructure behind the cloud is invisible; all you see are the applications and documents you use, not the technology that drives access.

Should You Buy a Chromebook?

Given all the various portable computing choices available today—Windows notebooks, Mac notebooks, and iOS and Android tablets—is a Chromebook the right device for you?

As with any technology purchase, you need to weigh the pros and cons, and then decide what's best for your own personal use. With that in mind, let's take a look at the benefits and disadvantages you might find in using a Chromebook running Chrome OS.

HP Chromebook 14

Chromebook Pros

For many users, a Chromebook is a viable alternative to other portable computing devices available today. There are many advantages to using a Chromebook over a Windows or Mac computer, including the following:

- **Price**—With numerous models in the $199–$299 price range, Chromebooks are price-competitive with lower-priced Windows notebooks—and much lower-priced than comparable Mac notebooks. Yes, there are higher-priced Chromebooks available, but a $200 model runs all the same apps just as fast as one priced two to three times that. (The more expensive ones, however, typically have larger screens, touch-screens, and more flexible configurations, which you may want to pay a little more for.)

- **No software to buy**—Not only does a Chromebook cost less than a comparable Windows or Mac notebook, you also don't have to lay out big bucks for software to run on the device. Because a Chromebook doesn't run traditional (and expensive) computer software, you instead load a variety of free or low-cost web-based apps. Considering the high price of Microsoft Office and similar programs, you can save hundreds or even thousands of dollars by using web-based applications. That also means you don't have to worry about installing multiple programs, or managing regular upgrades; with web apps, there's nothing to install, and all upgrades happen automatically.

- **No worry about local storage and backup**—With a traditional computer, you have to manage limited hard disk storage space and worry about backing up your important files. Not so with a Chromebook; all your files are stored on the Web, where you have virtually unlimited storage, so you don't have to worry about data storage at all. You also don't have to worry about backups because you always have a copy of your files online.

- **Reduced malware danger**—Because you don't download and run traditional computer software, computer viruses and spyware are virtual non-issues on a Chromebook. You don't even have to run antivirus programs, because viruses simply can't be installed on Chrome OS.

- **Enhanced security**—If you lose a traditional computer, all your personal files and information is also lost—or, in the case of theft, placed in the hands of criminals. Not so with a Chromebook. If somebody steals your Chromebook, all they get is a piece of hardware; because all files and data are stored on the Web, nothing important resides on the machine itself. This makes a Chromebook the most secure computer available today.

- **Faster boot up**—Instant resumption from sleep mode. Reboot from scratch in less than 10 seconds. Try to find a Windows-based computer that can do that.

- **Automatic updates**—Chrome OS is a cloud-based operating system, which means it's automatically and constantly updated whenever you connect to the Internet. The updates are small and frequent, unlike the large and intrusive updates to Windows, as an example.

- **Longer battery life**—Since Chromebooks run very efficiently (and don't have to drive CD/DVD drives and hard drives), they have significantly longer battery life than a typical notebook PC. All Chromebooks have at least an 8-hour battery life, with some models lasting 12 hours or longer on a single charge.

- **Enhanced collaboration**—Cloud computing is built for collaboration. Because your documents are all stored on the Web, multiple users can access and edit those documents in real time. No more passing files around from user to user—all you have to do is use your Chromebook to go online and start collaborating.

- **Ideal for multiple users**—With traditional computing, every user has to have his own computer, which stores all his files and personalized computing environment. With Chrome OS, your files, applications, and personalized desktop are stored on the Web; any Chromebook you use becomes your personal Chromebook once you log in to your Google account. A single Chromebook can easily be shared between multiple users, and it really doesn't matter whose computer it is.

- **Multiple form factors**—While there was just one original Chromebook model, today there are models in all sorts of configurations. You can find screen sizes from small (11.6") to large (15.6"), some with touchscreens, and some in a "convertible" format where the keyboard either folds over or detaches so you can use the screen like the tablet. That also means you'll find Chromebooks at a variety of price points, from $150 or so all the way up to $1,000. Whatever type of Chromebook you want, you can find.

Lenovo C330 convertible 2-in-1 touchscreen Chromebook

Chromebook Cons

While a Chromebook is the ideal portable computing device for most users today, it's not the right choice for everyone. In particular, Chromebooks have the following drawbacks:

- **They don't run Windows.** If you're used to Microsoft's Windows environment, Chrome OS might take a bit of getting used to. If you really, really don't want to leave Windows behind, a Chromebook is not for you.

- **They don't run Microsoft Office.** Many businesses and other organizations are standardized on Microsoft Office apps—Word, Excel, and the like. Although there are web-based versions of these Office apps, these aren't quite as robust as the traditional desktop software. If you absolutely, positively must use the desktop version of Microsoft Office, stick with a Windows PC.

- **They're not great for multimedia editing.** If you do a lot of photo or video editing, a Chromebook probably isn't going to be your ideal choice. Chromebooks don't have the heavy-duty processing power as the Windows or (especially) Mac computers that the pros prefer, plus there currently aren't web-based versions of the most-used multimedia editing tools, such as Adobe Creative Cloud or Final Cut Pro.

- **They're not great for gaming.** Likewise, Chromebooks are not the best machines for serious gamers. They just don't have the processing or graphics power—and can't run any disc-based games. Better to stick with a Windows gaming PC.

- **They don't work offline.** Chrome OS relies on an Internet connection to run web-based apps, so there's not a lot you can do with a Chromebook if there's no Internet connection handy. If you don't have access to a fast and reliable Internet connection, stick with a traditional Windows or Mac computer.

In other words, if you need a powerful computer to run demanding desktop software and games, a Chromebook will disappoint. For just about anything else, however, a Chromebook will do the trick—and at a lower price than a comparable Windows or Mac machine!

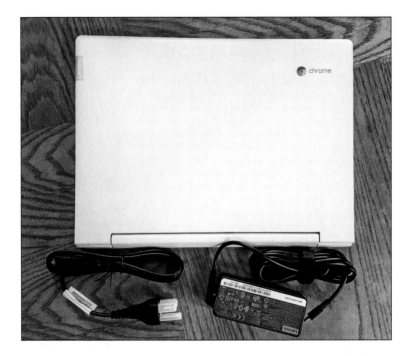

In this chapter, you learn what you need to do to start using your new Chromebook.

→ Unboxing Your Chromebook
→ Turning On Your Chromebook—For the Very First Time

2

Unboxing and Setting Up Your New Chromebook

Setting up a new Windows or Mac computer can be a daunting process. There are all sorts of questions to answer and configurations to make. It's typically a process that takes a half hour or more, and no one likes doing it.

Setting up a new Chromebook is different. The unboxing and setup process typically takes less than 5 minutes, and there's really not much to it. Read on to learn what you need to do.

Unboxing Your Chromebook

A typical Chromebook is a simple affair. Even the box itself is simple—small, lightweight, and, believe it or not, easy to open.

What do you find when you open the box? Here's what most manufacturers pack inside:

- The Chromebook, wrapped for protection

- AC adapter and power cable

- Quick start guide (and sometimes an instruction manual)

That's it. Obviously, there are no software or operating system disks because all of that is handled over the Internet. (And, as an added bonus, a Chromebook does not come with trial software versions or "crapware" preinstalled; you get a very clean desktop on first boot up.)

Turning On Your Chromebook—For the Very First Time

Google claims that it takes less than a minute to set up a new Chromebook. It might take a few minutes longer than that, but you get the idea. It's a relatively fast and painless process, as you'll see.

Charging the Battery

Out of the box, it's likely that your Chromebook's battery is not fully charged. For that reason, you need to plug it in to an external power source during initial setup and then leave your Chromebook plugged in for several hours to charge the battery.

Connect Your Chromebook

Before you use your new Chromebook, you need to unbox it and plug it in.

Google Account

Setup is easiest if you have a working Google Account before you first set up your new Chromebook. Although you can create a new Google Account during the setup process, it goes a lot faster if you can just enter your Google Account username and password. (If you use Gmail or any other Google service, you already have a Google account.) You can create a (free) Google Account from any web browser on any computer; just go to accounts.google.com and follow the onscreen instructions.

1. Remove the Chromebook and the other components from the box.

2. Connect the AC adapter to the power cable.

3. Connect the AC adapter to the power connector on the back or side of the Chromebook.

4. Plug the power cable into a working power outlet.

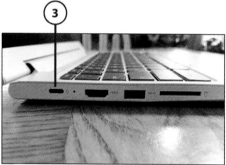

Set Up Your Chromebook

Once your Chromebook is plugged in, it's time to start it up and set it up.

1. Open the Chromebook.

2. Press the Power button, which will be either on the side of computer or on the keyboard.

3. When the Welcome screen appears, select your language from the list and select any Accessibility settings you want.

4. Click Let's Go.

5. Select your wireless network from the list.

6. Click Next.

Wireless Connections

Learn more about managing Wi-Fi connections in Chapter 6, "Connecting to Home Networks and the Internet."

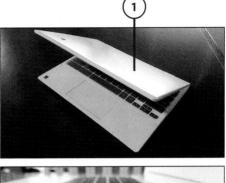

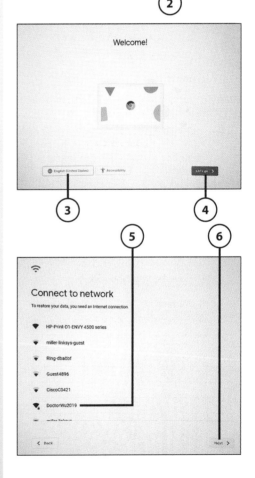

7. When the Join Wi-Fi Network window appears, enter your network password.

8. Click Connect.

Secure Networks

Most home wireless networks are secure networks, which means you need to supply the appropriate password to access them. In contrast, many public wireless networks are open networks, which means no password is necessary to gain access.

9. Read the Google Chrome OS Terms and then click the Accept and Continue button.

10. Chrome checks for operating system updates. This may take several minutes. (You see the Please Wait screen while this happens.) When the update is complete, your Chromebook restarts. After restarting, your Chromebook displays the Sign In to Your Chromebook window.

11. If you do not yet have a Google Account, click More Options and follow the onscreen instructions to create a new account.

12. If you already have a Google Account, enter your email address or phone number.

13. Click Next.

14. Enter your password.

15. Click Next.

16. You are signed in. All your existing Chrome bookmarks, browsing history, passwords, and other settings are automatically synced to your new Chromebook. Click Accept and Continue.

17. You're prompted to read the terms of service for the Google Play Store. Click More to view the entire document.

Google

Hi Michael

molehillgroup@gmail.com

Enter your password

Forgot password?   Next

⑭   ⑮

G

You're signed in!

Chrome sync
Your bookmarks, history, passwords, and other settings will be synced to your Google Account so you can use them on all your devices.

Personalize Google services
Google may use your browsing history to personalize Search, ads, and other Google services. You can change this anytime at myaccount.google.com/activitycontrols/search

☐ Review sync options following setup

Accept and continue

⑯

Google Play apps and services
Use Google Play to install Android apps

Google Play

Google Play Terms of Service
February 5, 2018

Google privacy policy

Send system data. This device currently automatically sends diagnostic and device and app usage data to Google. You can change this at any time in your device settings. If you turned on additional Web & App Activity, this information will be stored with your account so you can manage it in My Activity. Learn More

☑ Back up to Google Drive. Easily restore your data or switch device at any time. Your backup includes app data. Learn More

Skip   More

⑰

18. When you're done reading, click I Agree.

19. Google Chrome launches and displays the Howdy screen. Click the Take a Tour button to view a short walkthrough of your new Chromebook's most important features. Or...

20. Click the X at the top-right corner to close this window and start using your Chromebook right now.

Set It and Forget It

You only need to set up your Chromebook once. After you've completed this initial setup, you go directly to the login screen each time you start it up.

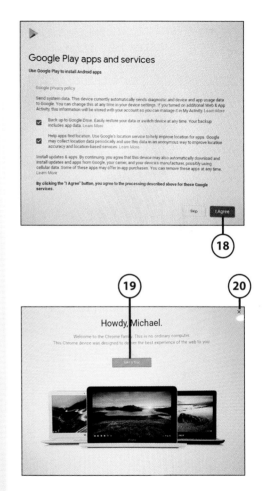

In this chapter, you learn how to recognize the various pieces and parts of your new Chromebook, as well as how to use the keyboard and touchpad.

Getting to Know Your Chromebook

A Chromebook looks much like a traditional notebook computer. The lid opens to show the LCD display and keyboard, and there are ports and connectors and such along all sides of the case.

Before you use your Chromebook, you need to know what all these items are and what they do. You'll also want to get to know the Chromebook's keyboard and touchpad, which are a bit different from those found on other computers.

Understanding the Parts of a Chromebook

A Chromebook is like a simplified version of a traditional notebook computer. There are fewer ports and connectors, and even fewer keys on the keyboard and touchpad. That makes it easier to operate—if you know where everything is located.

Different Models, Different Manufacturers

Although the keyboard and main operating controls are similar among the different models, different manufacturers include different sets of ports on their Chromebooks—and put them in different places. Consult your Chromebook's operating manual (often found on the manufacturer's website) for specific instructions.

What's Not Included

Because a Chromebook is streamlined by design, it lacks some of the connections found in a traditional Windows or Mac computer. For example, there is no Ethernet port, no CD/DVD drive, and no microphone input.

Screen

When you open the Chromebook case, the screen is the first thing you see. This is an LCD screen, typically backlit, for decent viewing, even under bright light. Some Chromebooks have touchscreens, which let you use your fingers to tap onscreen buttons and such.

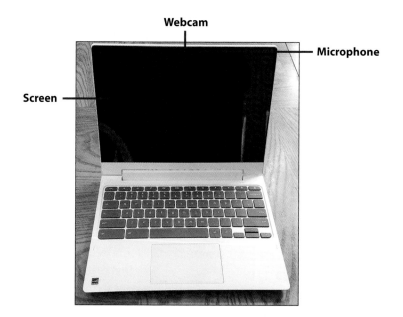

Webcam

All Chromebooks come with a built-in camera, also known as a *webcam*. The webcam is typically located directly above the screen, in the middle of the frame. You can use the webcam to conduct video chats and conferences, make video calls, create recorded videos, and take still photographs of yourself.

When you're using the webcam, the webcam's operating LED lights up. This LED is located next to the webcam, above the Chromebook's screen.

Microphone

The Chromebook's microphone is also typically located above the screen, either to the left or right of the webcam. It is used to capture audio during video chats, conferences, calls, and recordings. You can also use it for audio chats and Internet phone calls.

Keyboard

The keyboard is located on the base of the Chromebook. It's a little different from a traditional Windows or Mac keyboard; nonessential keys have been removed, and web-specific keys have been added. Learn more about the Chromebook's keyboard in the "Using the Keyboard" section, later in this chapter.

Keyboard

Touchpad

Touchpad

The Chromebook's touchpad is located directly below the primary keyboard. It functions as your Chromebook's mouse and cursor controller. Note that the touchpad does not include a right- or left-click button; instead, you tap the touchpad itself to click. Learn more in the "Using the Touchpad" section, later in this chapter.

Headset Jack

You'll find a headset jack on either the front or side of the Chromebook. Use this jack to connect a headset or earbuds for listening to your Chromebook's audio.

Memory Card Slot

Some Chromebooks include a slot for solid-state memory cards, like those used in digital cameras. This is typically a multicard slot, capable of accepting different types of cards—SD, SDHC, SDXC, Micro SD, and so forth.

Some Chromebooks put the memory card slot on the left or right side of the case, some in the rear. You can use this slot to access photos from a digital camera, digital audio files, or even stored video files.

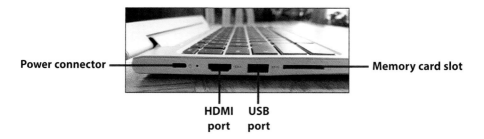

USB Port

Most Chromebooks have one or more USB ports. You can use these ports to connect any USB devices to your Chromebook.

HDMI Connector

Many Chromebooks feature an HDMI connector either on the rear or side of the unit. Use this connector to connect your Chromebook to a TV or audio/video receiver; it transmits both HD video and audio from your Chromebook.

Status Indicator

On either the front or rear of the Chromebook (sometimes next to the power connector), you should see a small LED light that serves as a status indicator. This indicator typically glows green when the Chromebook is running on external power and the battery is fully charged; it glows red when running on external power and the battery is being charged; and it is off when the computer is running on battery power.

Power Connector

The final item on the back or side of most Chromebooks is the power connector. This is where you connect the power adapter to your Chromebook for external power.

Convertible Chromebooks

So-called "convertible" Chromebooks that fold the keyboard into a tablet configuration may have additional controls on one side. My Lenovo convertible, for example, has volume and power buttons on the right side, along with the headphone jack.

Using the Keyboard

The Chromebook keyboard is a simplified version of a traditional computer keyboard. It's simplified in that several lesser-used keys are missing; this lets your Chromebook make the remaining keys bigger in a smaller space.

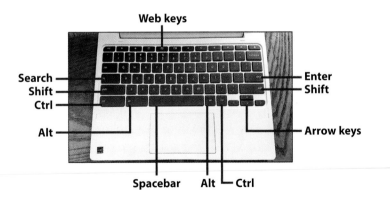

The first keys that are missing are the traditional function (F1, F2, F3, and so on) keys normally found on the top row of the keyboard. In place of these function keys, Chromebooks typically feature a row of "web keys" that perform specific functions for web browsing. The following table describes these web keys on most Chromebook keyboards.

Web Key	Function
	Go to the previous page in your browser history
	Go to the next page in your browser history
	Reload the current page
	Open the current page in full-screen mode
	Switch to next window
	Decrease screen brightness
	Increase screen brightness
	Mute/unmute the audio
	Decrease the volume
	Increase the volume

There's also an Esc key on the far-left side of this row.

Beneath the top row of web keys is the expected row of numeric (1, 2, 3, and so on) keys. This row also includes the Backspace key, which deletes the previous character entered.

The next three rows contain the traditional alphabetic (A, B, C, and so on) keys. At the ends of these rows are your Chromebook's Shift, Ctrl, Alt, and Enter keys, along with a grouping of four arrow keys for navigation.

Note that there is no Caps Lock key on the Chromebook; if you need to type capital letters, you'll need to hold down the Shift key as necessary (at least on some models; some manufacturers go with a slightly different keyboard layout that still includes the Caps Lock key).

Where you might expect to find a Caps Lock key is a new Chrome-specific Search key. Press this key to go to the address bar on the New Tab page to initiate a web search.

It's Not All Good

What's Missing?

If you're used to a traditional Windows or Mac computer, you'll find several keys missing from the Chromebook keyboard. Here are the keys you're used to that aren't on the Chromebook:

- F1–F12 function keys
- Caps Lock
- Insert
- Delete
- Home
- End
- Page Down
- Page Up
- Windows
- Menu

>>>Go Further

TURN THE SEARCH KEY INTO A CAPS LOCK KEY

You can, with a little work, turn Chrome's Search key into a Caps Lock key. Click the System Tray (where the time and date are) at the bottom right of the screen, and then click Settings. When the Settings page appears, go to the Device section and click Keyboard Settings. Pull down the Search list and select Caps Lock instead of the default Search.

You can further customize your keyboard by remapping the Ctrl, Alt, Esc, and Backspace keys in the same fashion.

Using the Touchpad

Just below the keyboard is your Chromebook's touchpad, which provides the same functionality as an external mouse. That is, you use the touchpad to move the onscreen cursor and click and select items onscreen.

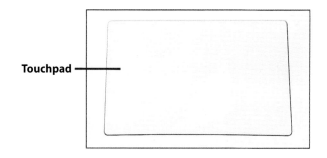

Touchpad

External Mouse

If you don't like the touchpad, you can connect an external mouse to one of the Chromebook's USB ports. See the "Connecting External Devices" section, later in this chapter, to learn how.

Move the Cursor

You use your finger on the touchpad to move the cursor around the Chromebook screen.

1. Place your finger lightly on the touchpad.

2. Move your finger in the direction in which you want to move the cursor.

The mouse cursor moves in the direction you moved your finger.

Click the Cursor

There are two ways to click an item onscreen, both of which use the touchpad.

1. Move the cursor on top of the item to click.

2. Tap your finger anywhere on the touchpad.

To double-click an item, tap twice instead of once.

Right-Click the Cursor

Many useful functions often appear via a pop-up menu when you right-click an item onscreen. But how do you right-click a touchpad that doesn't have a right button?

1. Move the cursor to the item on which you want to right-click.

2. Place two fingers anywhere on the touchpad and tap once.

Drag an Item

To move an item to another position on screen, you drag it to a new position.

1. Move the cursor to the item you want to move.

2. Press and hold the touchpad while you drag the item to a new location.

3. Lift your finger from the touchpad to "drop" the item in place.

Scroll the Screen

If you're viewing a long web page or editing a long document, you need to scroll down the screen to see the entire page. Although you can do this with the keyboard's up-arrow and down-arrow keys, you can also scroll with the touchpad.

1. Place two fingers lightly on the touchpad, but do *not* press down on the touchpad.

2. Drag your fingers down to scroll down the page.

3. Drag your fingers up to scroll up the page.

>>>Go Further

PAGE SCROLLING

On a traditional notebook PC, you can scroll up or down one page at a time by using the Page Up and Page Down keys. Unfortunately, there are no Page Up and Page Down keys on a Chromebook keyboard, so that option is not available. You can, however, press the Alt+Up Arrow and Alt+Down Arrow key combinations to scroll up or down one page at a time. You can also press the Spacebar to scroll down a page.

Adjust Touchpad Sensitivity

If you find that your touchpad is too sensitive, or not sensitive enough, you can adjust the sensitivity of the touchpad.

1. Click the bottom-right area of the screen (called the System Tray) to display the Quick Settings panel.

2. Select Settings.

3. Go to the Device section and click Touchpad.

4. Drag the Touchpad Speed slider to the left (Slow) to make it less sensitive, or to the right (Fast) to make it more sensitive.

Tap-to-Click

By default, you click within the touch area of the touchpad to click an onscreen item. If you'd prefer to press in the touch area instead, open the Touchpad section of the Settings panel and then turn "off" the Enable Tap-to-Click switch.

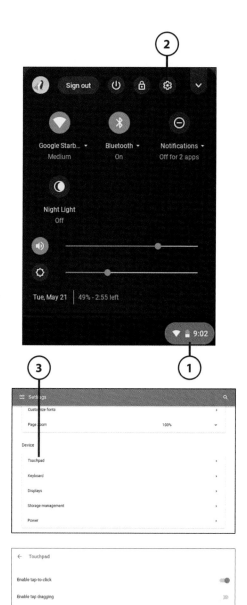

Connecting External Devices

Although a Chromebook is a relatively self-contained unit, you can connect various external devices to the machine, typically via USB.

Connect an External Mouse

If you don't like your Chromebook's built-in touchpad, you can connect an external mouse to one of the USB ports. You can connect either a corded or cordless model.

1. Plug the wireless receiver for a wireless mouse into one of the Chromebook's USB ports. (If you're connecting a wired mouse, connect the mouse's cable into the USB port.)

2. Your Chromebook should immediately recognize the external mouse and make it available for use.

Connect an External Keyboard

You can also connect a larger external keyboard to your Chromebook via USB. As with an external mouse, you can connect either a corded or cordless keyboard.

1. Connect the cable from the external keyboard to one of the Chromebook's USB ports. (If you're connecting a wireless keyboard, plug the wireless receiver into the USB port.)

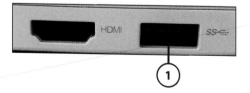

2. Your Chromebook should immediately recognize the external keyboard and make it available for use.

Connect to a TV

If you're watching streaming movies or television programs, the
typical Chromebook screen doesn't
deliver a big-screen viewing experience. Fortunately, you can use your
Chromebook to deliver streaming
Internet programming to your living
room TV—and watch it all on the big
screen.

1. Connect one end of an HDMI
   cable to the HDMI connector on
   your Chromebook.

2. Connect the other end of the
   HDMI cable to an HDMI input on
   your television set or audio/video
   receiver.

3. Switch your TV or receiver to the
   proper HDMI input.

   You should see on your television
   screen whatever is playing on
   your Chromebook.

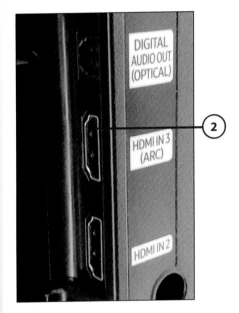

External Storage
You can also connect certain
external storage devices to your
Chromebook via USB. Learn more
in Chapter 9, "Managing Files and
Using External Storage."

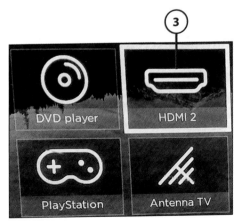

Adjusting Brightness and Volume

Your Chromebook includes dedicated keys, located in the top row of the keyboard, for adjusting screen brightness and audio volume.

Adjust Screen Brightness

You can make your Chromebook display brighter or darker. A brighter display may look nicer, especially under bright lighting, but it can drain the battery faster. Dimming the screen a tad can still look good while maximizing battery life.

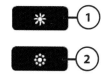

1. To increase screen brightness, press the Increase Brightness key.

2. To decrease screen brightness, press the Decrease Brightness key.

One press of either key changes the brightness by one level.

>>>Go Further
CLEANING THE SCREEN

It's important to keep your Chromebook's LCD screen clean. You should clean the screen with a soft cloth, lightly moistened with a special computer cleansing fluid. You can find this fluid at any consumer electronics or computer supply store. Squirt the fluid directly on your cleaning cloth and then lightly wipe the screen in a single direction; using too much force can damage the screen.

Adjust and Mute the Volume

Whether you're using your Chromebook's built-in speaker or listening through headphones or earbuds, you'll probably need to adjust the volume level at some point.

1. To increase the volume level, press the Increase Volume key.

2. To decrease the volume level, press the Decrease Volume key.

3. To mute the volume, press the Mute button; press the button again to unmute the sound.

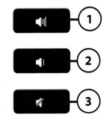

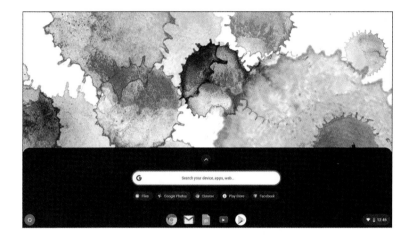

In this chapter, you learn how to turn your Chromebook on and off, how to navigate the desktop, and how to enter and emerge from sleep mode.

→ Starting Up and Shutting Down
→ Navigating the Chrome OS Desktop
→ Navigating Chrome Windows
→ Using Touchscreen Gestures

Using Chrome OS and the Chrome Desktop

Using a Chromebook is similar to using a traditional notebook computer, but faster. Because less operating system overhead is involved, as well as fewer internal components, a Chromebook boots up much quicker than a Windows or Mac machine; it wakes up from sleep mode almost immediately.

What you find after you start up your Chromebook, however, may not be totally familiar to you, especially if you're used to using a Windows or Mac notebook. To use your Chromebook, you need to get used to the Chrome OS interface.

Starting Up and Shutting Down

The most basic computer operations are turning the computer on and turning it off. Your Chromebook should start up in less than 10 seconds, and power down almost immediately.

Start Up and Log In

Your Chromebook can be run either on battery power or from a connection to an external AC power source. Once it powers up, you have to log in to the computer with your username and password.

1. To power up your Chromebook, simply open the case and lift the LCD display panel. *Or…*

2. If the display panel is already open, press the Power button. (This may be either on the keyboard or on the side of the unit.)

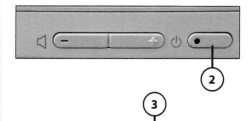

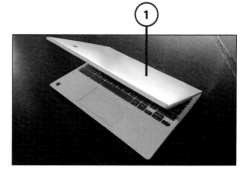

Power Button

The small LCD on the Power button lights when your Chromebook is turned on.

3. When the login screen appears, click to select your user account (if you have more than one account on this machine). Otherwise, just accept your default account and move to step 4.

4. Enter your password.

5. Press Enter or click the right arrow.

   Google Chrome launches and displays the desktop.

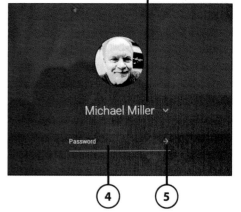

Put Your Chromebook to Sleep

Although you can completely power off your Chromebook, you may prefer to enter sleep mode instead. This is good for when you're not actively using the Chromebook for a period of time but expect to resume use soon; it conserves your Chromebook's battery life.

The advantage of sleep mode over powering down your Chromebook is that when you're ready to resume use, your Chromebook resumes operation immediately. If you instead opt to power down and then restart your Chromebook, you'll have to sit through the (admittedly short) startup process and then reenter your password.

Turning Off the Screen

Your Chromebook automatically turns off its screen after six minutes of inactivity (eight minutes if you're using external power). You redisplay the screen by swiping across the touchpad or pressing any key on the keyboard.

1. To enter sleep mode, close the lid of your Chromebook.

2. To wake up from sleep mode, open the lid of your Chromebook.

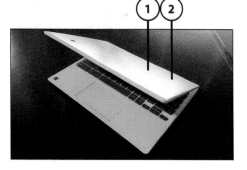

Power Off Your Chromebook

Shutting off your Chromebook is a simple matter of pressing the Power button. Unlike other operating systems, Chrome OS does not require a menu operation to power off.

1. Press and hold the Power button for 2 seconds to display the shutdown panel.

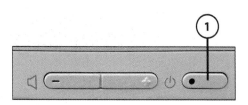

2. Click Power Off.

Your Chromebook now completely powers off. You can restart your Chromebook by following the startup procedure previously described.

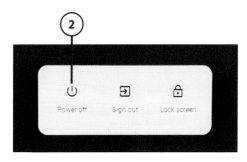

Locking the Screen

Chrome OS features a screen lock mode that displays the Chrome login screen. To access screen lock mode, press and hold the Power button for 2 seconds to display the shutdown panel; then click Lock Screen. To resume normal operation, select your username, enter your password, and then press Enter. To power off from screen lock mode, simply close the Chromebook's lid.

It's Not All Good

Forcing Shutdown

If for some reason your Chromebook freezes or refuses to shut down normally, you can force a shutdown by pressing and holding the Power button for at least 8 seconds.

Navigating the Chrome OS Desktop

Chrome OS features a desktop interface that looks and feels similar to the Windows or Mac OS desktop. You can open multiple windows to appear on the desktop, and size and arrange those windows as you like.

Browse the Shelf

Along the bottom edge of the desktop is the Shelf, which is kind of like the taskbar in Windows. This area contains icons for your most popular applications. By default, the Shelf hosts icons for the Launcher, Google Chrome, Gmail, Google Docs, YouTube, and the Google Play Store; you can also pin other apps to the Shelf. Click an icon to launch that app in a new window.

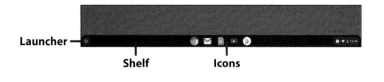

Launcher

Shelf   Icons

Google Play Store

Learn more about Chrome apps and the Google Play Store in Chapter 11, "Using Chrome and Android Apps."

>>>Go Further

MOVE OR HIDE THE SHELF

By default, the Shelf appears at the bottom of the screen. You can, however, move the Shelf to either side of the screen, where it appears vertically. To move the Shelf, right-click anywhere in the Shelf at the bottom of the screen (by tapping the touchpad with two fingers), click Shelf Position, and then select Left, Bottom, or Right.

You also can autohide the Shelf so that it isn't always taking up valuable screen real estate. In this mode, the Shelf stays hidden until you move your cursor to the bottom of the screen.

To autohide the Shelf, right-click at the bottom of the screen and then check Autohide Shelf. To deactivate the autohide feature, right-click the bottom of the screen and uncheck Autohide Shelf.

Open the App Drawer

The first icon in the Shelf is the Launcher. You use the Launcher to open the App Drawer, which is kind of like Chrome's version of the Windows Start menu.

1. Click the Launcher icon (or, on a touchscreen display, use your finger to drag the Shelf up).

2. You see the initial App Drawer panel. This panel includes a search panel, which you can use to search for apps and files on your Chromebook, as well as icons for your most recently opened apps. Click an app to reopen it.

3. Click the up arrow at the top of the App Drawer (or, on a touch-screen display, drag up the top of the App Drawer) to make the App Drawer fill the entire screen.

4. The full-screen version of the App Drawer provides access to all the apps installed on your Chromebook. Click any icon to launch that app.

5. If you have a lot of apps installed, the full-screen App Drawer takes up multiple pages. Click one of the round icons on the right side of the screen to display another page full of apps. (Or, on a touch-screen Chromebook, use your finger to scroll from one page to the next.)

6. To close either version of the App Drawer, click the Launcher icon again.

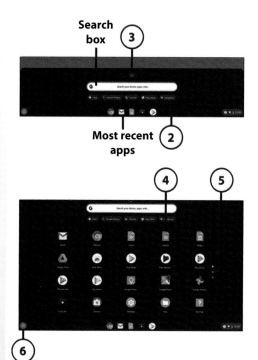

Search box ③

Most recent ② apps

④ ⑤

⑥

Organize the App Drawer

If you have multiple pages of apps, you might want to organize your App Drawer so that your most-used apps are grouped together. You can move app icons to new locations and group multiple icons into folders.

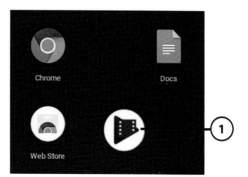

1. To move an icon, use your touchpad or touchscreen to drag and drop it into a new location. As you move an icon to a new position, all icons after that one will be scooted to the right.

2. To create a new folder, drag an icon and drop it on top of another.

3. Both icons are now in the newly created folder. Click to open that folder.

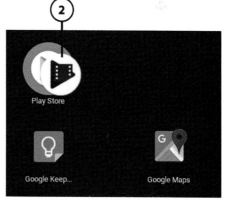

4. To add another icon to the folder, just drag it onto the folder icon or into the open folder.

5. To name a folder, enter a name into the Unnamed field.

6. To remove an icon from a folder, open the folder and drag the icon out.

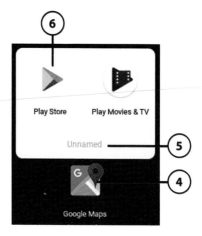

View the System Tray

At the far right of the Shelf is an area called the System Tray. The System Tray includes information about your system and access to your personal settings.

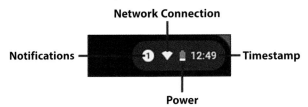

Network Connection

Notifications — 🔔 ▼ 🔋 12:49 — **Timestamp**

Power

The four main status icons in the status area are Notifications, Network Connection (Wi-Fi), Power (battery level or AC), and Timestamp (date and time)—although you may see other icons, depending on the given situation.

Configure Settings with the Quick Settings Panel

Many of the most commonly used Chrome system settings can be configured from the Quick Settings panel, which you access from the System Tray.

1. Click anywhere on the System Tray to display the Quick Settings panel.

2. Notifications are displayed at the top of the Quick Settings panel. Click or (on a touchscreen display) swipe a notification to move to the next one.

3. Click Power to turn off your Chromebook.

4. Click Lock to lock your Chromebook.

5. Click Settings to display the Settings window, which lets you configure more system settings.

Chrome OS Settings
Learn more about configuring the Chrome OS settings in Chapter 8, "Configuring and Personalizing Chrome OS."

6. Click Wi-Fi to view and switch to other Wi-Fi networks.

7. Click Bluetooth to turn Bluetooth wireless connectivity on or off.

8. Click Notifications to configure notification settings.

9. Click Night Light to turn on or off Night Light mode.

10. Drag the Volume slider to raise or lower your Chromebook's volume level.

11. Drag the Brightness slider to increase or decrease screen brightness.

12. Click the down arrow to hide the Quick Settings panel.

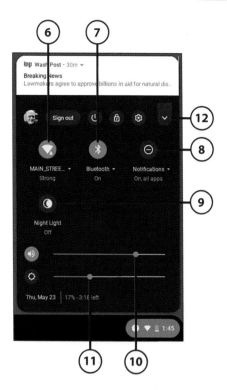

Navigating Chrome Windows

Every app you open in Chrome appears either in its own window or as a tab in a Chrome browser window.

Open a New Chrome Window

If no window is currently open, you can open a new window by clicking the Chrome icon on the Shelf. You can open multiple windows at the same time on the Chrome desktop.

>>>Go Further

CREATE A NEW WINDOW FROM A TAB

You can drag any currently open tab from the Chrome browser window to the Chrome desktop. This opens a new window for the page or app in that tab.

Manage Window Size

It's easy to change the size of any open window on the desktop.

1. To minimize a window to the Shelf, click the Minimize button.

2. To maximize a window, so that it appears full screen, click the Maximize button on the top-right corner of the window. Alternatively, press the Full Screen button on the Chromebook keyboard.

3. To return a maximized window to its previous size, click the Maximize button again.

4. To resize a window, mouse over any window edge or corner until the cursor changes shape; then drag the cursor to resize the window.

5. To dock a window to the left side of the screen, drag the window's title bar to the left side of the screen.

6. To dock a window to the right side of the screen, drag the window's title bar to the right side of the screen.

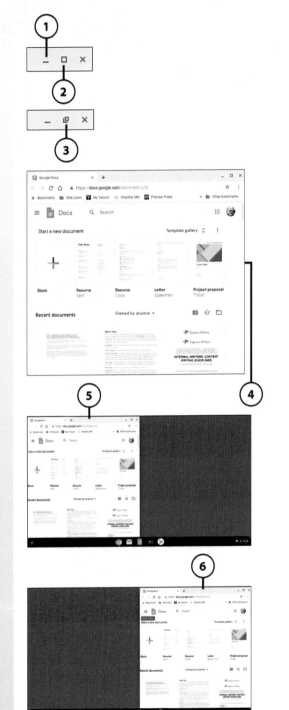

Switch Between Open Windows

Chrome lets you open multiple windows and then switch between windows. There are two ways to switch to the next open window in Chrome.

1. Press the Next Window button on the top row of your Chromebook's keyboard. *Or…*

2. Press Alt+Tab on the Chromebook keyboard to display the switcher panel, and then select the window you want to use (not shown).

Switching Tabs

To switch between tabs in an open browser window, press Ctrl+Tab.

Close a Window

Closing any open window is a one-click operation:

Click the X at the top right of the window.

Click to close the window

Using Touchscreen Gestures

Many newer Chromebooks come with touchscreen displays. This is particularly useful if you have a convertible Chromebook that you can also use as a tablet.

To take full advantage of a touchscreen display, you need to master various touchscreen gestures. The following table details some of the more useful ones.

Chrome Touchscreen Gestures

Action	Gesture
Click	Tap where you want to click
Close a window	Swipe down from the top of the window
Display the App Drawer	Swipe up from the Shelf at the bottom of the screen
Go to a previous page	Swipe your finger left to right
Go to the next page	Swipe your finger right to left
Hide the App Drawer	Swipe down from the top of the App Drawer
Right-click	Touch and hold where you want to right-click
Scroll	Drag your finger in the direction you want to scroll
View all open windows	Swipe down from the top of the screen
Zoom in	Spread your fingers apart
Zoom out	Pinch your fingers together

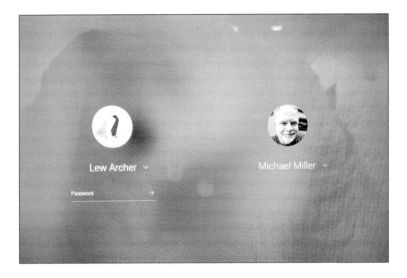

Lew Archer ∨

Password →

Michael Miller ∨

In this chapter, you learn how to create multiple users for your Chromebook, how to switch from user to user, and how to edit your account picture and information.

→ Adding and Switching Users
→ Editing User Information

Managing Multiple Users

A Chromebook is only a piece of hardware; all of your personal settings, information, and data are stored online. As such, you can log in to any Chromebook machine with your Google Account, and it'll look and work just like your own Chromebook. It's easy enough for other users to log in to your Chromebook, as well, and make it their own.

How easy is it to add new users to a Chromebook? Pretty easy, as you'll soon discover.

Adding and Switching Users

When you first set up your Chromebook, you were prompted to enter your Google Account name and password. This account becomes your default user account on your Chromebook. You can, however, add other users to your Chromebook—that is, let other people with Google Accounts use this particular Chromebook.

Add a User

You can let any number of users log on to your Chromebook, as long as they all have Google Accounts.

1. Click the System Tray to display the Quick Settings panel.

2. Click Sign Out.

3. From the login screen, click Add Person.

4. When the Sign In to Your Chromebook screen appears, enter the new user's Gmail address.

5. Click Next.

6. Enter the user's Gmail password.

7. Click Next.

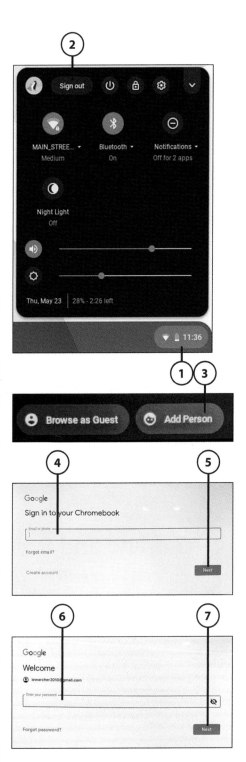

8. You're now signed in. Click Accept and Continue.

9. You're prompted to read the terms of service for the Google Play Store. Click More to view the entire document.

10. When you're done reading, click Accept.

Install Your Apps

If you use this new account on other devices, you might be prompted to install apps you use with those devices on this Chromebook. You can choose to do so if you like.

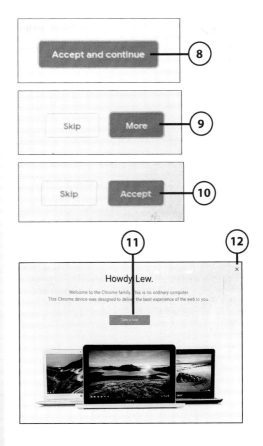

11. Google Chrome launches and displays the Howdy screen. Click the Take a Tour button to view a short walkthrough of your new Chromebook's most important features. Or...

12. Click the X at the top-right corner to close this window and start using your Chromebook right now.

>>>Go Further
USING OTHER CHROMEBOOKS

With the Chrome OS, you're not limited to a single Chromebook. You can also use other people's Chromebooks by logging in to your Google Account on those machines.

When you log in to any Chromebook with your Google Account, that Chromebook displays all the apps and personalization you've made to your own Chromebook. In essence, your Chromebook settings travel from machine to machine; they're tied to your account in the cloud, not to any particular piece of hardware.

Switch User Accounts

If you've created multiple user accounts for your Chromebook, it's easy to switch from one user account to another—without shutting down your machine.

1. Click anywhere in the System Tray to display the Quick Settings panel.

2. Click your profile picture.

3. If another user is already signed in, click to switch to that user. *Or…*

4. To switch to a user that is not already signed in, open the Quick Settings panel and click Sign Out.

5. Click the user account you want to switch to.

6. Enter that user's password, and then press Enter or click the right arrow.

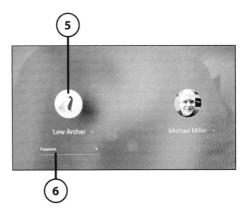

Log In as a Guest User

Any person can log in to your Chromebook as a Guest user. A Guest user has limited use of the Chromebook; he or she can browse the Internet, but not save or access files on your machine. In addition, a Guest user's browsing and search history are not saved.

1. Start up your Chromebook or sign out of a currently running account.

2. Your Chromebook displays the login screen. Click Browse as Guest.

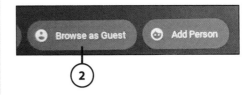

Editing User Information

Don't like the picture you've chosen for your Chromebook user account? It's easy enough to change—along with other information in your Google Account.

Change Your Profile Picture

Google Chrome lets you choose from a selection of built-in icons for your user account picture, upload an existing picture, or shoot a new picture using your webcam.

1. Click anywhere in the System Tray to display the Quick Settings panel.

2. Click Settings.

3. When the Settings window appears, scroll to the People section and click your account name.

4. From the Change Picture panel, click one of the icons to use for your picture. *Or...*

5. To take a picture with your Chromebook's webcam and use it for your account picture, click the Camera icon. When the live image from your webcam appears, smile into the camera and click the Take Photo button. If you like the picture that results, click the OK button. *Or...*

6. To upload a stored picture for your account picture, click the Folder icon. When the Select a File to Open panel appears, navigate to and select the file you want to upload and then click the Open button.

7. Click the X to close the window (not shown).

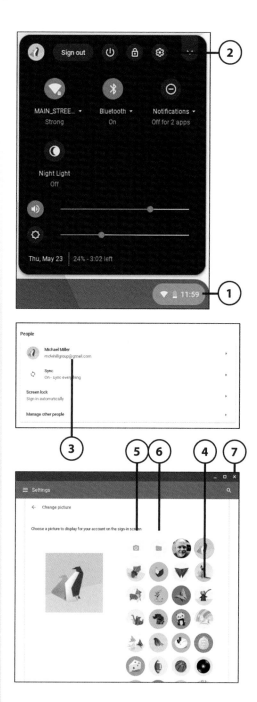

Edit Your Profile

Your Chromebook account is tied to your Google Account, in that they both use the same username (email address) and password. This lets you log in to your account from any Chromebook.

Your Google Account is used by all Google services and applications, and includes your personal account profile. If this is a new Google Account, you need to create a new profile. You can also edit your profile at any time.

1. Click the Chrome icon on the Shelf to open a new Chrome window.

2. Go to www.google.com (this page may open by default) and click your account name or picture in the top-right corner of the page.

3. Click the Google Account button.

4. Click Personal Info to edit your personal information.

5. Click the item you want to edit.

6. Click the pencil icon to edit that item.

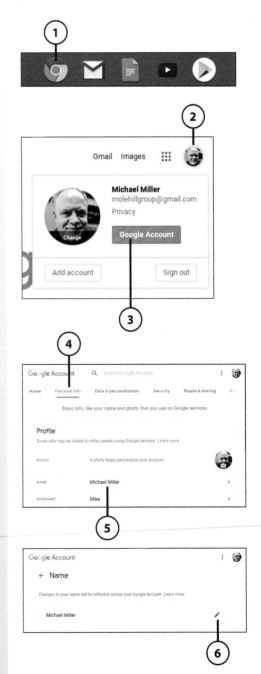

7. Enter the appropriate information for that item.

8. Click the Done or Update button (when available) when you're done entering information for that section.

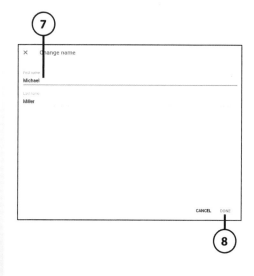

Google Account

A single Google Account provides access to all Google's various sites and services. That includes personalized search results from Google's search engine (www.google.com), email service from Gmail (mail.google.com), and online calendars on Google Calendar (www.google.com/calendar/).

6

Connecting to Home Networks and the Internet

Chrome OS is a web-based operating system; to fully use your Chromebook, you must be connected to the Internet. All Chromebooks include built-in Wi-Fi wireless connectivity, so you can connect to the Internet over any nearby Wi-Fi network. And, despite the Chromebook being primarily a portable device, it's also possible to connect a Chromebook to a wired network to access the Internet. Which option you use depends on your own specific circumstances.

Connecting to a Wi-Fi Network

Most users connect their Chromebooks to the Internet via some sort of Wi-Fi wireless connection. Wi-Fi is Chrome's default connection method, as most homes and offices are set up with Wi-Fi connectivity; also, numerous public Wi-Fi hotspots are available at coffee houses, libraries, hotels, restaurants, and the like.

Supported Networks
The current generation of Chromebooks can connect to 802.11 a/b/g/n and 802.11ac Wi-Fi networks, using all the popular wireless security protocols.

View Network Status

The Network icon in the status area at the bottom right of the Chrome desktop indicates the status of your Wi-Fi connection, as detailed in the following table.

Wi-Fi Status Icons

Icon	Status
▼	Connected to a Wi-Fi network
▼	No Wi-Fi connection

Enable Wi-Fi on Your Chromebook

Wi-Fi connectivity is enabled by default on most Chromebooks. If necessary, however, you can enable Wi-Fi manually.

1. Click anywhere in the System Tray to display the Quick Settings panel.

2. Click Not Connected.

3. Click "on" the Wi-Fi switch to display a list of available networks.

Disabling Wi-Fi

If Wi-Fi is enabled, you can disable Wi-Fi by opening the Quick Settings panel and switching "off" the Wi-Fi switch.

Connect to an Open Wi-Fi Network

Once Wi-Fi is enabled on your Chromebook, connecting to a Wi-Fi network is as easy as selecting the network from a list. Many Wi-Fi networks (especially public ones) are "open," in that anyone can connect without supplying a password.

1. Click anywhere in the System Tray to display the Quick Settings panel.

2. Click Not Connected.

3. Chrome displays a list of nearby available wireless networks. Open networks are marked with a regular wireless icon; private networks (those that require passwords to access) have a lock next to the icon. Click the open network to which you want to connect.

   The network name is now displayed with the word "Connecting" next to it. When "Connecting" disappears, you're connected.

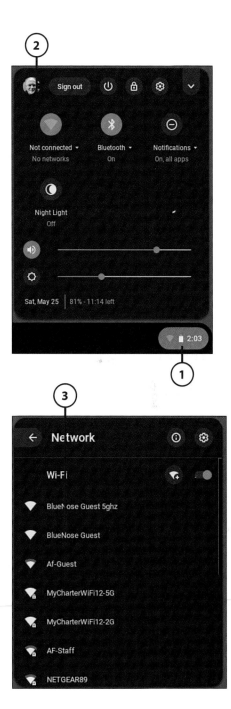

>>>Go Further

PUBLIC NETWORKS

Some public Wi-Fi networks, such as those you find in a coffee shop or hotel, may require additional login information after you've connected to the network. In most instances, a proprietary login screen will appear when you first attempt to view a website; you'll then need to follow the onscreen instructions to connect.

For example, when you connect to the Wi-Fi at a Starbucks, you first connect to the open Google Starbucks or ATTWIFI network. (Starbucks uses different Wi-Fi providers in different locations.) The first time you connect, you'll be prompted to log in to the network. Click this prompt to open the Chrome browser, with the network's log-in page displayed. Click the Accept and Connect button to accept the terms and conditions and connect to the network.

In other instances, such as at some hotels, you may be asked to provide a password provided by the establishment when you first use your web browser. If the Wi-Fi service isn't free, you may also be asked to provide a credit card for billing, or approve billing to your room number.

Connect to a Secure Wi-Fi Network

Many Wi-Fi networks, especially home and business networks, are secure, in that they require a password for access. You'll need to supply this password to connect to a secure network.

1. Click anywhere in the System Tray to display the Quick Settings panel.

2. Click Not Connected.

3. Chrome displays a list of nearby available wireless networks. Secure networks (those that require a password for access) are marked with a "locked" icon. Click the network to which you want to connect.

4. Chrome displays the Join Wi-Fi Network dialog box; enter the password for the network.

5. Click the Connect button to connect.

>>>*Go Further*

CONNECTING VIA ETHERNET

In some instances, you'll get better performance by making a wired connection to your network instead of a wireless one. An Ethernet connection is both faster and more stable than a Wi-Fi connection; it's also more secure, virtually immune to outside hacking.

Because the Chromebook is designed to be a wireless device, however, connecting via Ethernet is a secondary option. In fact, most Chromebooks don't include Ethernet ports, which means you'll probably need to purchase an external USB Ethernet adapter that plugs in to a USB port on your computer.

If your Chromebook has an Ethernet port (or if you've connected a USB Ethernet adapter), all you have to do is connect one end of an Ethernet cable to your Chromebook and the other end to your network router. The Network icon in the status area changes to an Ethernet icon and indicates the status of your connection.

Managing Network Connections

If you connect to the Internet in different locations, chances are you connect through a variety of different wireless networks. Managing your available wireless networks, then, is important.

Automatically Connect to a Network

If you have a favorite wireless network at a given location where multiple networks may be available, you can configure your Chromebook to automatically connect to your network of choice.

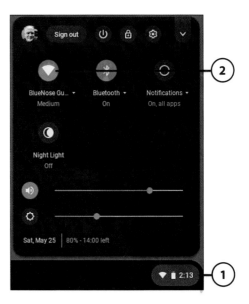

1. Make sure you're connected to the network in question; then click anywhere in the System Tray to display the Quick Settings panel.

2. Click the Wi-Fi icon for the network you're connected to. The panel changes.

3. Click the currently connected network to display the Settings panel for that network.

4. Switch "on" the Automatically Connect to This Network switch.

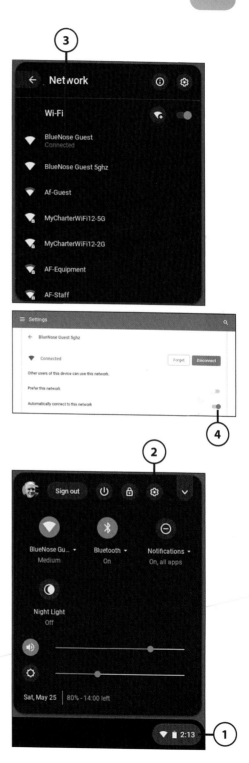

Forget a Network

Chrome automatically saves details about each and every network you connect to. If there is a network to which it's unlikely you'll ever connect again, you can clear the details for that network—in effect, you tell Chrome to forget that network.

1. Click anywhere in the System Tray to display the Quick Settings panel.

2. Click Settings.

3. When the Settings window appears, go to the Wi-Fi section and click the current network.

4. In the Known Networks list, click the network you want to forget.

5. Click the Forget button.

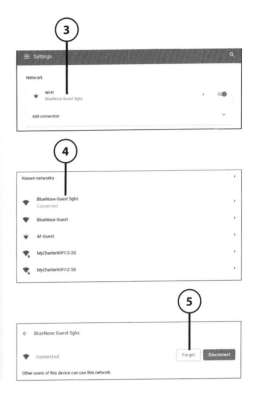

>>>Go Further
NO HOME NETWORKING

The Chromebook is designed as an Internet device; it's not a networking computer. Even though you connect to the Internet via a wireless network, you can't access other devices on the network.

This means you can't use your Chromebook to access other computers connected to the network, share files stored on the network, or access a network printer. For that matter, other network computers can't see or access your Chromebook, even when it's connected through a given network.

The only way to share files with other network users is to access those files via a cloud-based service, such as Google Drive, or email the files using Gmail.

In this chapter, you learn how to use Google Chrome to browse and search the Web.

→ Browsing the Web
→ Viewing and Managing Browser History
→ Managing Your Home Page
→ Bookmarking Favorite Pages

Using the Chrome Browser

The Google Chrome OS is built around Google's Chrome web browser, the most popular browser in use today. To get full use of your Chromebook, you need to master the Chrome browser.

Browsing the Web

Google's Chrome web browser is integrated into the Chrome OS interface. You use the Chrome browser to access all web-based apps, as well as most system settings.

Go to a Web Page

One of the quickest ways to browse the Web is to go directly to a given web page. You do this by entering the page's address, or URL, into Chrome's Omnibox—the big text box at the top of the browser window.

Omnibox

What other browsers call an Address box, Chrome calls the Omnibox. That's because it's more than a simple Address box; you can also use it to enter queries for web searches. When you start typing in the Omnibox, Google suggests both likely web pages and search queries. Just select what you want from the list or finish typing your URL or query; then press Enter.

1. Type a web page's URL into the Omnibox at the top of the Chrome window.

2. As you start typing in the Omnibox, Google suggests both queries and web pages you are likely to visit. Select the page you want from the drop-down list.

3. Alternatively, finish typing your URL and press Enter.

    Chrome navigates to and displays the page you entered.

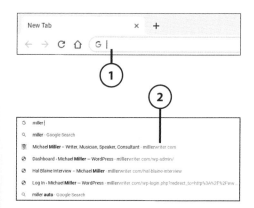

Click a Link

Another way to navigate the web is to click a link (technically called a *hyperlink*) you find on a web page. Most text links are in color or underlined; buttons or pictures can also be links. The cursor typically changes shape when you hover over a link.

Clicking a link takes you directly to the linked-to page. You can open links in the current browser tab or, if you prefer to keep the current page visible, in a new tab or window.

- To open the link in the current tab, click the link.

- To open the link in a new tab, move the cursor to the link, right-click the link (tap two fingers once on the touchpad), and select Open Link in New Tab.

- To open the link in a new window, move the cursor to the link, right-click the link (tap two fingers once on the touchpad), and select Open Link in New Window.

Reload a Page

If you stay on a web page too long, you may miss updates to that page's content. In addition, if a page doesn't fully or properly load, you may need to "refresh" or reload that page:

Click the Reload This Page button to the left of the Omnibox.

Reload This Page button

Move Forward and Back Through Pages

You can easily revisit pages you've previously displayed, and then move forward again through visited pages.

1. To move backward through previously visited pages, click the Back button.

2. To move forward through pages, click the Forward button.

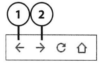

Zoom In to a Page

If you're having trouble reading small text on a page, Chrome lets you increase the zoom level to make that text bigger. You can also decrease the zoom level to make the entire page smaller.

1. Click the Customize and Control button at the top right to display the drop-down menu.

2. To increase the zoom level, go to the Zoom section of the menu and click the + button.

3. To decrease the zoom level, go to the Zoom section of the menu and click the – button.

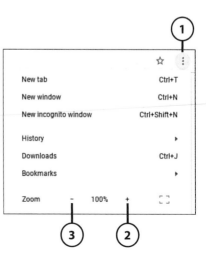

Browse in Incognito Mode

Google Chrome, like most web browsers, keeps a record of every web page you visit. That's fine, but every now and then you might browse some web pages that you don't want tracked.

If you want or need to keep your browsing private, Google Chrome offers what it calls Incognito mode. In this special mode (actually, a separate browser window), the pages you visit aren't saved to your browser's history file, cookies aren't saved, and your activity is basically done without any record being kept.

Simultaneous Windows

Chrome lets you run both normal and Incognito windows simultaneously.

1. Click the Customize and Control button to display the drop-down menu.

2. Click New Incognito Window.

3. This opens a new Incognito window, recognizable by the little spy icon next to the first tab. You can switch between the Incognito and other open windows by pressing the Next Window button on your Chromebook's keyboard. When you are finished browsing in Incognito mode, click the X in the window's tab to close it.

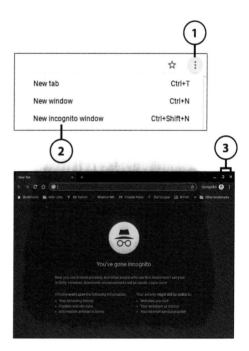

Viewing and Managing Browser History

Another way to revisit web pages you have viewed in the past is to use Google Chrome's history feature.

View Your Recent History

Chrome keeps track of your history for up to 90 days.

1. Click and hold the Back button.

2. This displays a list of pages you've visited in your current browsing session. To revisit a specific page, click it in the list.

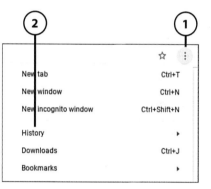

View Your Full History

To revisit pages viewed on other days, you can access your full browsing history.

1. Click the Customize and Control button to display the drop-down menu.

2. Click History.

3. The History panel displays. To revisit any particular page, click that page's link.

4. To view your complete history, click History.

Other Devices

The History page displays your browser history across all devices that share your Google account, so you may see browser history from your Chromebook, smartphone, tablet, and other computers.

Delete Browsing History

You may not want your entire browsing history visible to others using your Chromebook—or accessing your Chrome browser on another computer. To that end, you can delete your browsing history—as well as other "tracks" to your web browsing.

Chrome lets you delete the history of web pages you've visited, files you've downloaded, cookies, and other data from websites. You can even empty the browser cache, clear saved passwords, and clear automatically filled form data.

Cache and Cookies
The *cache* is a local storehouse of recently visited pages. A *cookie* is a small file, stored on your computer, that certain websites use to track your browsing behavior.

You can clear any of these items stored in the past hour, the past day, the past week, the past four weeks, or from the beginning of time (or at least when you started using your Chromebook).

It's Not All Good

Don't Clear Everything

You may not want to select all the options in the Clear Browsing Data dialog box. Clearing browsing and download data erases your browsing history, so those are probably good choices. Emptying the cache is sometimes necessary, in and of itself, to clear out old versions of pages and enable you to see the most recent versions of some web pages. Deleting cookies is generally not advised, however, because this will get rid of tracking data that make some sites easier to access. And clearing saved passwords and Autofill form data might also make it less convenient to revisit pages where you've previously entered information.

1. Click the Customize and Control button to display the drop-down menu.

2. Select More Tools.

3. Click Clear Browsing Data to display the Clear Browsing Data dialog box.

4. Click either the Basic or Advanced tab and check those items you want to delete or clear.

5. Pull down the Time Range list and select how much data to delete.

6. Click the Clear Data button.

Managing Your Home Page

The Home page is the page that opens when you first launch the browser.

Choose a New Startup Page

By default, Chrome displays the New Tab page when you open the browser. You can, however, change what displays on launch.

1. From within the Chrome browser, click the Customize and Control button.

2. Select Settings.

3. Scroll to the On Startup section and select what you want to happen when you start your Chromebook:

   - Open the New Tab page

   - Continue where you left off (display the last opened page)

   - Open a specific page or set of pages (you'll then get to select)

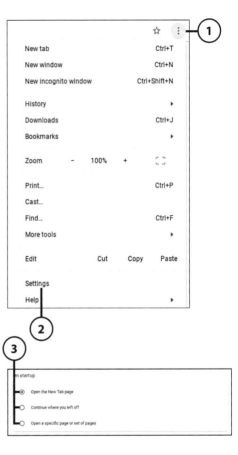

Customize the Home Button

Chrome can display a Home button, next to the Omnibox, that opens a selected page when clicked. This button may not be displayed by default, so you may need to enable it—and then select what page opens when you click it.

1. From within the Settings window, scroll to the Appearance section.

2. Switch "on" the Show Home Button switch.

3. Select which page you want to display when you click the Home button:

   - New Tab page

   - Custom web address (you have to enter the URL for the page you want)

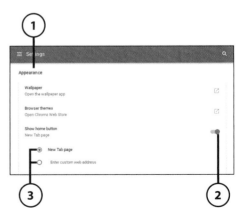

Bookmarking Favorite Pages

Google Chrome lets you keep track of your favorite web pages via the use of *bookmarks*. You can bookmark the pages you want to return to in the future and display your bookmarks in a Bookmarks bar that appears just below Chrome's Omnibox.

Bookmark a Web Page

There are several ways to bookmark a web page. This is the fastest method.

1. Navigate to the web page you want to bookmark.

2. Click the Bookmark This Page (star) icon in the Omnibox.

3. Chrome displays the Bookmark Added box. Edit the name of the bookmark, if you want.

4. Pull down the Folder list to determine where you want to save this bookmark.

5. Click the Done button to save the bookmark.

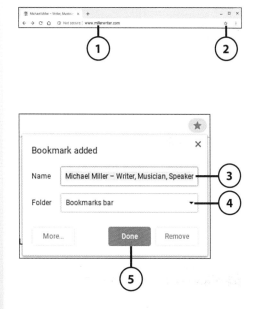

Display the Bookmarks Bar

You can view your bookmarks by clicking the Customize and Control button and selecting Bookmarks. Or you can display a Bookmarks bar beneath Chrome's Omnibox. You'll need to enable this manually.

1. Click the Customize and Control button to display the drop-down menu.

2. Select Bookmarks.

3. Click Show Bookmarks Bar.

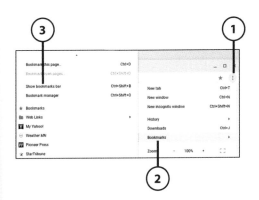

Manage Bookmarks

Google Chrome lets you organize your bookmarks into folders and subfolders that branch off from the Bookmarks bar, as well as in other folders on the same level as the Bookmarks bar. You do this by using Chrome's Bookmark Manager.

1. Click the Customize and Control button to display the drop-down menu.

2. Select Bookmarks, Bookmark Manager.

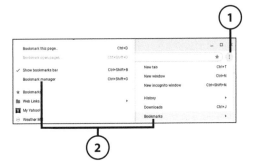

3. When the Bookmark Manager tab opens, the folders and subfolders of bookmarks are displayed in the left navigation pane; the individual bookmarks are displayed in the right pane. To display the contents of a folder or subfolder, select that folder in the navigation pane.

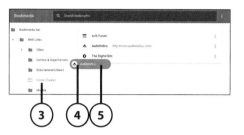

4. Change the order of bookmarks in a folder by clicking and dragging that bookmark to a new position.

5. Move a bookmark to a different folder by dragging and dropping that bookmark onto the new folder.

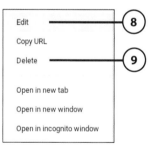

6. To list a folder's bookmarks in alphabetical order, select the folder, click the Organize (three-dot) button on the menu bar, and then select Sort By Name.

7. To create a new folder or subfolder, click the Organize (three-dot) button and select Add New Folder.

8. To edit information about a specific bookmark, select the bookmark, click the Organize (three-dot) button by that bookmark, and then select Edit. Then you can edit the bookmark's name and URL from within the URL list.

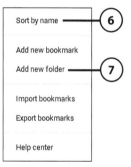

9. To delete a bookmark, select that bookmark, click the Organize (three-dot) button by that book-mark, and select Delete.

>>>Go Further

BOOKMARKS WITHOUT THE BAR

If you don't want to display the Bookmarks bar, there are other ways to access your bookmarks.

First, any time you display the New Tab page, the Bookmarks bar is displayed (along with thumbnails of recently visited pages). Just open a new tab and proceed from there.

You can also access your bookmarks from the Customize and Control menu. Click the Customize and Control button and then click Bookmarks; all your bookmarks are now displayed.

In this chapter, you learn about the many configuration options available with Chrome OS,
from changing Chrome's startup behavior to
selecting a new desktop background.

Configuring and Personalizing Chrome OS

Chrome OS works just fine in its default configuration, but there are
a lot of things about Chrome you can configure to create a more
uniquely personal user experience.

Personalizing the Desktop

You can customize the Chrome OS desktop in terms of colors and
background images. It's a quick and easy way to personalize your
Chrome experience.

Change the Desktop Wallpaper

Most users like to select their own pictures for their computer desktops. It's no different with Chromebooks, which is why Chrome OS offers the option of personalized background images. You can select from images provided by Google, images uploaded from your computer, or plain colored backgrounds.

1. Click anywhere in the System Tray to display the Quick Settings panel.

2. Click Settings.

3. Go to the Appearance section of the Settings window and click Wallpaper to open the Wallpaper window.

From the Desktop

You can also display the Wallpaper window by right-clicking anywhere on the open desktop (by tapping with two fingers once on the touchpad) and selecting Set Wallpaper.

4. Select a tab to display wallpapers of a given type—Cityscapes, Landscapes, Earth, Abstract, and so forth.

5. Click the wallpaper you want to use. This image is now downloaded to your computer and set as your desktop background.

6. Click the X to close the panel.

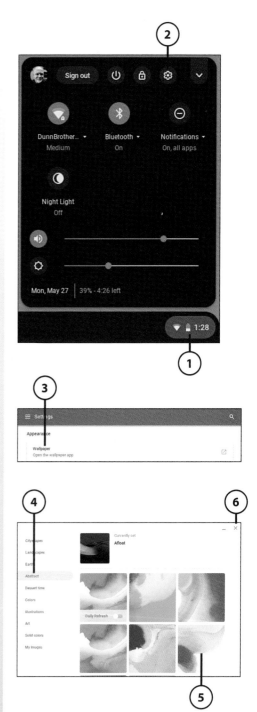

Daily Refresh

Some wallpaper categories show an option for Daily Refresh. When you switch "on" this option, you see a new wallpaper each day from within that category.

Configuring Other Settings

There's more you can customize about Google Chrome, all accessible from the Settings window—which you get to by clicking anywhere in the System Tray and then clicking Settings. (Some settings may only be visible when you click Show Advanced Settings at the bottom of the window.)

Configure the Touchpad

Don't like the way your Chromebook's touchpad works or feels? Then change it.

1. In the Settings window, go to the Device section and click Touchpad.

2. To disable tap-to-click functionality (which requires you to tap only at the bottom area of the touchpad), turn "off" the Enable Tap-to-Click switch.

3. To enable tap dragging on the touchpad, switch "on" the Enable Tap Dragging switch.

4. To change the sensitivity of the touchpad, adjust the Touchpad Speed slider.

Remap Key Functions

As previously noted, the Chromebook keyboard does not include some familiar keys, such as the Caps Lock key. You can, however, reconfigure how the Search, Ctrl, Alt, Esc, and Backspace keys work in Chrome—and thus turn these keys into other keys that you might be missing. You can also turn the top-row web keys into traditional function keys (F1, F2, F3, and so forth).

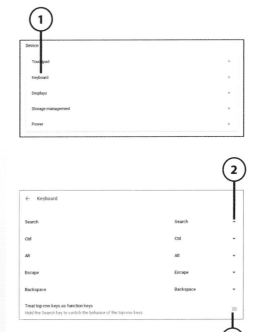

1. In the Settings window, go to the Device section and click Keyboard.

2. Pull down the list for the key you want to modify and make a new selection.

3. To turn the web keys into function keys, click "on" the Treat Top-Row Keys as Function Keys switch.

Manage Your Sync Settings

Chrome OS and the Chrome browser are part of Google's web-based cloud computing architecture. As such, if you use the Chrome browser on your smartphone or on another computer, you can configure Chrome to use the same bookmarks and settings on those other devices.

Synchronization is enabled by default on your Chromebook. You can, however, configure just what settings you want to sync across all your computers.

Synchronization

This synchronization between devices is possible because Google saves all your bookmarks and settings online in your Google Account. Whenever or wherever you launch Chrome and connect to your Google Account, the settings you see will be the same ones you saved previously. Any changes you make from any computer are also saved online, and those changes are visible from other computers you use to access the Internet. So after you get your Chromebook properly configured, the Chrome browser will look and feel the same on any other computer you use.

1. In the Settings window, go to the People section and click Sync.

2. By default, the Sync Everything switch is activated. To selectively sync individual settings, click this switch "off."

3. Switch "off" those apps you don't want to synchronize.

Disable Guest Browsing

Guest browsing is enabled by default in Chrome; this mode enables users not signed in to your computer to use it for basic tasks, such as browsing the Internet. If you'd rather not have unregistered users using your Chromebook, you can disable the guest browsing feature.

1. In the Settings window, go to the People section and click Manage Other People.

2. Switch "off" the Enable Guest Browsing switch.

Hide Usernames and Restrict Sign In

By default, you see the usernames and associated images for all users added to your Chromebook. You can, however, opt to hide these usernames and images. You can also restrict sign in only to those users you've selected.

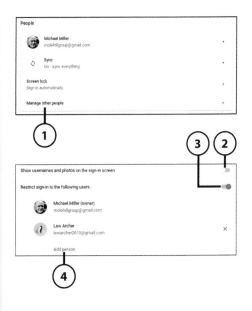

1. In the Settings window, go to the People section and click Manage Other People.

2. Switch "off" the Show Usernames and Photos on the Sign-In Screen switch.

3. Switch "on" the Restrict Sign-In to the Following Users switch.

4. To add another user to this list, click Add Person, enter that person's email address, and then click Add.

Change Your Time Zone

By default, Chrome determines the current date and time over the Internet. However, it might not know your exact location—especially when you're traveling. Fortunately, it's easy to change the time zone displayed in Chrome.

1. In the Settings window, click Advanced, go to the Date and Time section, and click Time Zone.

2. Check Choose from List.

3. Select your current time zone from the list.

Connect a Bluetooth Device

Many Chromebooks include built-in Bluetooth wireless, which is used to connect some wireless mice and keyboards. To connect an external Bluetooth device to your Chromebook, you may first have to enable your device's Bluetooth functionality. (This setting may be enabled by default.)

1. In the Settings window, go to the Bluetooth section and click Bluetooth.

2. Make sure the Bluetooth switch is clicked "on."

3. Your Chromebook automatically begins searching for nearby Bluetooth devices. When the new device is found, highlight it in the list and then follow the onscreen instructions to connect your Bluetooth device. You may be prompted to enter a PIN for the connected device.

Enable Autofill

If you do a lot of online shopping, you probably find yourself entering the same personal information on multiple shopping sites. You can simplify all this data entry by enabling Chrome's Autofill feature, which stores your basic information and enters it automatically whenever you encounter a similar form on a web page. You can have Chrome save your address and phone number, any credit cards you use, and passwords for the websites you visit.

1. In the Settings window, go to the Autofill section.

2. Click Passwords.

3. Switch "on" Offer to Save Passwords to be asked to save new passwords you enter.

4. Switch "on" Auto Sign-In to automatically sign in to websites where you've previously saved passwords.

5. To remove any saved password, click its More Actions (three-dot) icon and then click Remove.

6. Click the back arrow to return to the previous screen.

7. Click Payment Methods.

8. Click "on" Save and Fill Payment Methods to save payment data when entered.

9. To add a new payment method, click Add and follow the onscreen instructions.

10. To remove an existing payment method, click the Edit icon next to that entry and, when prompted, click Remove.

11. Click the back arrow to return to the previous screen.

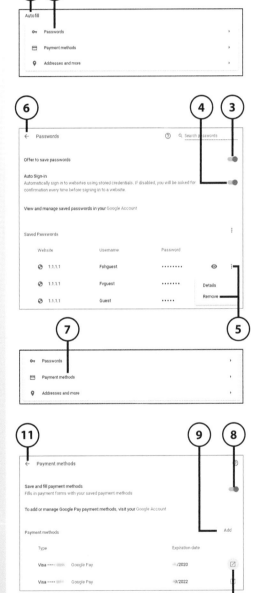

12. Click Addresses and More.

13. Click "on" Save and Fill Addresses to save address information you enter in the future.

14. To add a new address, click Add and follow the onscreen instructions.

15. To remove an existing address, click the More Actions (three-dot) icon and then click Remove.

Display Web Content

Chrome offers several options that determine how web pages are displayed in the browser. In particular, you can change the size and type of fonts used, as well as change the zoom level when viewing pages. You do all of this from Chrome's Settings window.

1. To change the size of the fonts used to display web pages, go to the Appearance section, pull down the Font Size list, and make a new selection from Very Small to Very Large. (Medium is the default size.)

2. To change the zoom level of the pages displayed, go to the Appearance section, pull down the Page Zoom list, and make a new selection.

3. To change the fonts used to display web pages, go to the Appearance section and click Customize Fonts.

4. To change the smallest size font displayed, adjust the Minimum Font Size slider.

5. To change the basic font, pull down the Standard Font list and make a new selection.

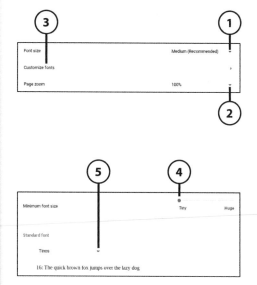

6. To change the serif font used, pull down the Serif Font list and make a new selection.

7. To change the sans serif font used, pull down the Sans-Serif Font list and make a new selection.

8. To change the fixed-width font used, pull down the Fixed-Width Font list and make a new selection.

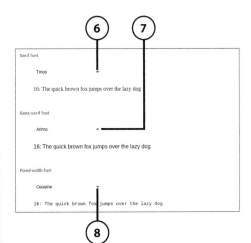

Customize Languages and Input Methods

By default, Chromebooks shipped in the U.S. display all menus and dialog boxes in English. If you speak another language, however, you can change this, and have Chrome display in a more familiar language.

You can also change the input method used for your Chromebook's keyboard. By default, Chrome uses a standard U.S. keyboard. You can opt instead to have your Chromebook mimic an international keyboard, extended keyboard, Dvorak keyboard, or others.

1. From the Settings window, click Advanced, scroll down to the Languages and Input section, and click Language.

2. Click Add Languages to add another display language. When the next dialog box appears, click the language you wish to use.

3. To change the keyboard input method, click Input Method.

4. Click Manage Input Methods.

5. Select a different keyboard.

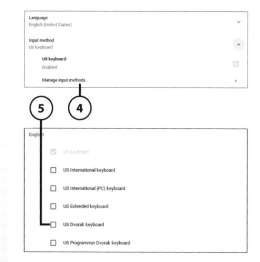

Manage Downloads

When you download files from the Internet, those files have to be stored somewhere. By default, that location is the Downloads folder—although that's something you can customize.

1. From the Settings window, click Advanced, go to the Downloads section, click the Change button next to Location, and then select a different folder.

2. If you want to be prompted for a new download location for each file, click "on" the Ask Where to Save Each File Before Downloading switch.

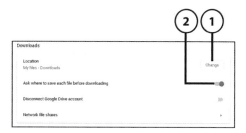

Disable Google Drive

Google Drive, Google's online storage service, shows up as a storage option when you're managing files on your Chromebook. You can, however, reconfigure Chrome so that you don't see Google Drive as an option.

1. Go to the Downloads section of the Settings window.

2. Click "on" the Disconnect Google Drive Account switch to not use Google Drive from the Files app. Or click the switch "off" if you want to use Google Drive from the Files app.

Enable Accessibility Features

If you have vision problems, using any operating system or web browser is difficult. Fortunately, Chrome includes several accessibility features that help you to find your way around the Chrome interface, all available in the Accessibility section of the Settings window. (You probably need to click Advanced in the Settings window to see this section.)

1. To display a menu of accessibility options on the Settings panel (when you click in the System Tray), click "on" the Always Show Accessibility Options in the System Menu switch.

2. To manage other accessibility options, such as text-to-speech, high contrast mode, and the onscreen keyboard, click Manage Accessibility Features and switch "on" any features you want to enable.

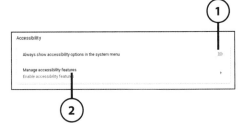

Reset to Default Settings

After you changed some of Chrome's
settings, you may want to revert back
to the original settings. You can do this
with the click of a button.

1. From the Settings window, click
   Advanced and scroll to the Reset
   Settings section.

2. Click Reset Settings to Their
   Original Defaults to reset your
   Chromebook's settings while
   keeping all existing accounts.

3. Click Powerwash to delete all user
   accounts and reset your entire
   Chromebook to out-of-the-box
   condition.

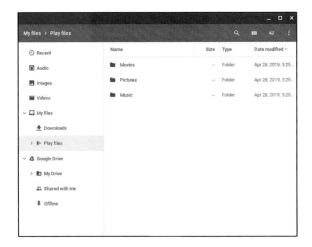

In this chapter, you learn how to manage stored and downloaded files on your Chromebook, and on external devices connected to your Chromebook.

9

Managing Files and Using External Storage

Your Chromebook is designed to be a cloud-based computing device. That is, it's designed to work with web-based applications and files stored on the Web. As such, most Chromebooks don't have much in the way of internal storage—a relatively meager 16GB to 32GB of solid state memory and no hard drive.

Although this is enough storage to hold the Chrome OS and a minimal number of pictures or other files you want to store locally, you may need additional storage space. Many people use the cloud-based storage of Google Drive (discussed in the next chapter), but you also can connect additional local storage with a USB memory stick or external hard drive. You manage all your local files with Chrome's built-in Files app.

Using the Files App

The Files app in Chrome OS is similar in concept to the file management utilities found in the Windows and Mac operating systems.

You can use the Files app to view, open, copy, cut, paste, and delete files stored on your Chromebook and on external devices connected to your Chromebook. It's relatively easy to access and quite easy to use.

To open the Files app, press Alt+Shift+M on your Chromebook keyboard. You can also open the Files app by clicking the Launcher to open the App Drawer and then click the Files icon.

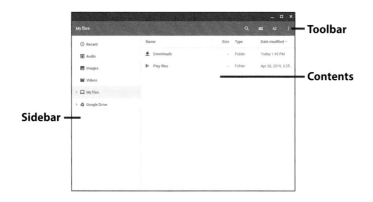

The Files app consists of two sections. The sidebar, on the left, organizes your files by type: Recent, Audio, Images, Videos, and My Files. It also displays any external storage devices you have connected and your online Google Drive storage. The main panel, on the right, displays the contents of the selected storage or folder. There's also a toolbar at the top, with controls relevant to the current selection.

The main panel can display contents either as a list or as large thumbnails. You select the file view by clicking either the List View or Thumbnail View icon in the toolbar.

Click for Thumbnail View

List View

In List View, the contents of the selected folder are displayed by default in reverse chronological order—that is, the most recent files first. For each file, you see the filename, size, type, and date modified. You can sort by any of these attributes by clicking the top of the selected column.

Click for List View

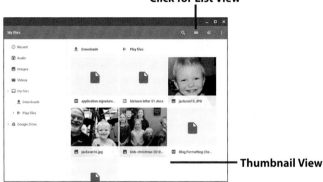

Thumbnail View

In Thumbnail View, you see only the name of the file, along with a thumbnail image of the file's contents. For a picture file, the thumbnail is the picture itself. For other types of files, the thumbnail image is more generic, and sometimes reflective of the file type.

On the left side of the toolbar at the top of the Files app is a "bread crumb" list of all the folders and subfolders in the path above the current folder. Click any folder or subfolder in this list to return directly to that folder.

Open Files and Folders

You have several ways to open files and folders from within the Files app.

- Click the file or folder and then click Open in the toolbar.

- Double-click the file or folder.

- Right-click the file or folder and then select Open.

- On a touchscreen display, tap the file.

Rename Files and Folders

You can, if you want, change the names of files from within the Files app.

1. From within the Files app, navigate to and right-click the file or folder you want to rename.

2. Select Rename from the pop-up menu.

Right-Clicking

To right-click using your Chromebook's touchpad, tap the touchpad once with two fingers.

---

3. The file or folder name is highlighted. Type the new name into the highlighted area and press Enter.

Copy a File

It's relatively easy to copy a file from its current location to another folder on your Chromebook, to an external storage device, or to your Google Drive.

1. From within the Files app, navigate to and right-click the file you want to copy.

2. Select Copy from the pop-up menu.

3. Navigate to the location where you want to copy the file and click the More (three-dot) icon.

4. Click Paste.

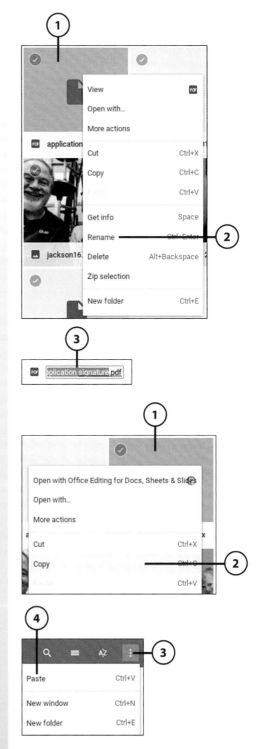

Move a File

Moving a file is different from copying it. When you copy a file, you leave the file in its original location, and paste a copy of that file to a new location; two files remain. When you move a file, via the cut-and-paste operation, the file is removed from its original location and pasted into the new location; only one file remains.

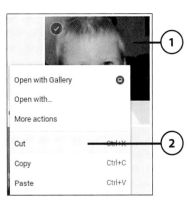

1. From within the Files app, navigate to and right-click the file you want to move.

2. Select Cut from the pop-up menu.

3. Navigate to the location where you want to move the file and click the More (three-dot) icon.

4. Click Paste.

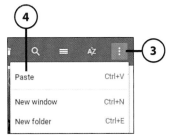

Delete Files

Naturally, the Files app lets you delete files and folders. This is often necessary to free up the limited storage space on your Chromebook.

1. Navigate to and click the file(s) or folder(s) you want to delete.

Selecting Multiple Files

You can select multiple files from within the Files app. Just check the box for each file you want to select, or hold down the Ctrl key while selecting multiple files.

2. Click Delete in the toolbar. Alternatively, you can right-click and select Delete from the pop-up menu.

Create a New Folder

To better organize your stored files, you can use the Files app to create multiple folders and subfolders.

1. Navigate to the folder where you want to add the new subfolder and click the More (three-dot) icon on the toolbar.

2. Click New Folder.

3. The Files app creates the new folder with the name area open for editing. Enter a name for the new folder and press Enter.

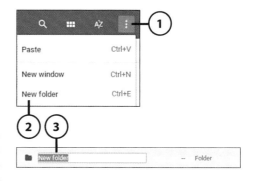

Save Files from the Web

Often, you'll find images and other files on websites that you'd like to save copies of. You can save these files directly to your Chromebook or to a memory card or external USB memory device connected to your Chromebook.

Limited Storage

Because your Chromebook has limited storage on board, you should probably save most downloaded files to an external storage device or to your Google Drive.

1. From within the Chrome browser, right-click the file or image you want to save and then select Save Image As or Save File As from the pop-up menu.

Open link in new tab

Open link in new window

Open link in incognito window

Save link as...

Copy link address

Open image in new tab

Save image as...

Copy image

2. When the Save File As window appears, select a folder in which to save the file.

3. Confirm or change the name of the file in the Filename field.

4. Click the Save button.

5. Chrome displays the Download Manager pane at the bottom of the browser window, and the file is downloaded.

Using External Storage Devices

You can connect various types of external file storage to your Chromebook. In particular, you can connect USB memory devices, memory cards (such as those used in digital cameras), and any external hard drive that connects via USB.

Connect a USB Memory Device

You can connect any USB memory device (sometimes called a flash drive or thumb drive) to your Chromebook's USB ports and then access data stored on the drive using the Files app.

1. Insert the USB memory device into an open USB port on your Chromebook.

2. Chrome recognizes the USB device, and displays the message "Removable Device Detected." Within this message, click Open Files App.

3. The Files app opens with the USB drive selected. Navigate within this device to find the file(s) you want.

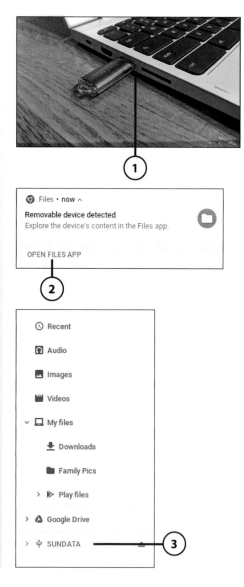

It's Not All Good

Ejecting an External Storage Device

While you can simply remove an external storage device when you're done with it, Chrome doesn't always like this—and sometimes scolds you about it! The better approach is to click the up arrow icon next to the device's name in the Files app; this "ejects" or disconnects the drive, which you can then safely remove by hand.

Insert a Memory Card

The memory card slot on most Chromebooks can read and write data to and from popular types of memory cards. These memory cards are typically used to store images taken from digital cameras. When you insert a memory card into your Chromebook, you can view the images stored on the card. You can also use memory cards to store files downloaded from the Internet.

1. Insert the memory card into the memory card slot on your Chromebook.

2. The Files app opens, with the memory card selected. Navigate within this device to find the file(s) you want.

Screen Captures

If you need to capture a picture of the current screen on your Chromebook, press the Ctrl+Next Window button. Screen captures are stored in the Downloads folder.

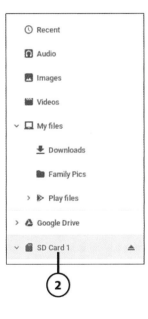

Connect an External Hard Drive

You can also connect an external USB hard drive to your Chromebook. This type of external drive lets you store more and larger files than you can with the Chromebook's internal storage; you can also use the external hard drive to store backup copies of your most important files.

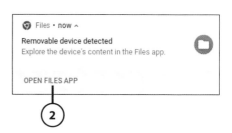

1. Connect the USB cable on the external drive to an open USB port on your Chromebook.

2. Chrome recognizes the external drive, and displays the message "Removable Device Detected." Within this message, click Open Files App.

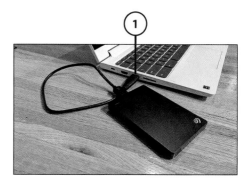

3. The Files app opens with the external drive selected. Navigate within this device to find the file(s) you want.

Name	Size	Type	Date modified ⌄
📁 Higher Standards	–	Folder	May 18, 2015, 2:13 PM
📁 TechSmith	--	Folder	Mar 28, 2015, 1:18 PM
📁 Work Files	–	Folder	Mar 27, 2015, 4:06 PM
📁 Notes	–	Folder	Nov 9, 2010, 4:20 PM
📄 Paragraphs.gdoc	–	Google docu...	Yesterday 12:37 PM
📋 Demographic Information [Form].gform	--	Google form	Yesterday 12:35 PM
📊 Demographic Information.gsheet	–	Google spre...	May 19, 2019, 11:26 ...
📄 mime-attachment.gdoc	–	Google docu...	Mar 11, 2019, 4:55 PM
📄 Collin mood.gdoc	--	Google docu...	Dec 21, 2018, 9:09 AM
📊 My Google Spreadsheet 1.gsheet	–	Google spre...	Dec 5, 2018, 8:31 AM
📊 My New Spreadsheet.gsheet	–	Google spre...	Dec 5, 2018, 1:12 AM
📄 text_0 (2).txt.gdoc	–	Google docu...	Apr 14, 2018, 9:15 PM

My Drive

Recent
Audio
Images
Videos
My files
  Downloads
  Family Pics
  Play files
Google Drive
  My Drive
  Shared with me
  Offline

In this chapter, you learn how to store your important files online using Google Drive.

→ Storing Files on Google Drive
→ Sharing with Google Drive

10

Using Google Drive to Store and Share Files

Chromebooks have minimal onboard storage space for files, no more than 32GB or 64GB in all, with many having just 16GB. With little local storage space available, then, where do you store your files? Online, of course—in the cloud.

Chrome OS was built on the concept of cloud-based file storage. To that end, Google recommends its Google Drive cloud storage service. Google Drive makes it easy to access your important files from any computer, in any location. Google Drive is also great for sharing files with friends, family, and co-workers.

Storing Files on Google Drive

Although you can manage your Google Drive files from the Google Drive web page (drive.google.com), it's easier to do so from within Chrome's Files app. Google Drive appears as a storage device in your Chromebook's Files app. You can copy files to and from Google Drive as you would to and from any storage device or location.

Files App

Learn more about using Chrome's Files app in Chapter 9, "Managing Files and Using External Storage."

View Your Google Drive Files

When you first sign up for Google Drive, you'll see a few "test" files in your main folder. You can delete these if you wish, and then begin using Google Drive to store additional files.

1. From within the Files app, go to the Google Drive section in the sidebar and click My Drive.

2. The contents of your main folder display; different types of files have distinctive icons. Click any subfolder to view those contents.

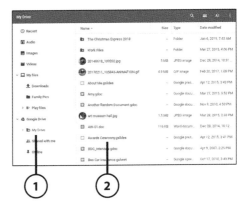

Copy a File to Google Drive

Copying a file from your Chromebook or external storage device to Google Drive is as easy as clicking and dragging.

1. From within the Files app, select the file you want to copy to Google Drive.

2. Click and drag the file to the My Drive icon in the sidebar. The cursor changes to a thumbnail of the file while you're dragging it.

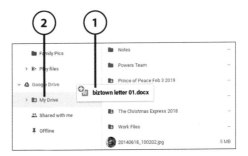

Copy and Paste

You can also copy a file to your Google Drive by right-clicking the file (tap with two fingers once on the touchpad) and selecting Copy; you then open your Google Drive folder, right-click, and select Paste.

Open a File from Google Drive

Opening a file stored on Google Drive is just like opening a file stored directly on your Chromebook.

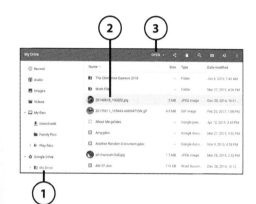

1. From within the Files app, click My Drive under Google Drive in the sidebar.

2. Click to select the file you want to open.

3. Click Open on the toolbar.

Delete Files from Google Drive

From time to time, it's good to free up space in your Google Drive folder by deleting old or unused files.

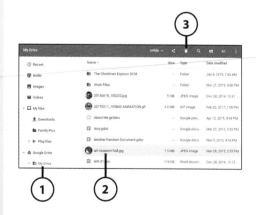

1. From within the Files app, click My Drive under Google Drive in the sidebar.

2. Click to select the file(s) you want to delete.

3. Click Delete in the toolbar. You will be asked if you're sure you want to delete the file. Click Delete.

Create a New Google Drive Folder

To better organize large numbers of files, you can create additional subfolders within your main Google Drive folder. You can use these subfolders to store specific types of files. For example, you might create a subfolder just for work files or for holiday pictures.

1. From within the Files app, click My Drive under Google Drive in the sidebar; then navigate to where you want to create the new subfolder.

2. Click the More (three-dot) icon in the toolbar.

3. Click New Folder.

4. Google Drive creates the new folder with the name area open for editing. Enter a name for the new folder and press Enter.

>>>Go Further

GOOGLE DRIVE STORAGE

By default, every user with a Google Account gets 15GB of free Google Drive storage. Even better, when you purchase a new Chromebook, Google gives you 100GB of Google Drive storage for 12 months. To redeem your 100GB free storage with a new Chromebook purchase, go to www.google.com/chromebook/offers/ and click the Redeem button.

If you need more storage space, you can purchase it from Google. An additional 100GB will cost you $1.99 per month; an additional 200GB costs $2.99 per month; an additional 2TB of storage runs $9.99 per month; 10TB costs $99.99 per month; and an excessively large 20TB runs $199.99 per month. Manage your Google Drive storage and purchase additional storage at www.one.google.com/storage.

Sharing with Google Drive

Google Drive cloud storage is ideal for when you want to share a file with someone. Perhaps you want to share pictures with friends or family, or even collaborate on a group project for work. All you have to do is tell Google Drive to share that file with selected people, and then they can view it from their computers or smartphones. (If you enable the proper access, they can edit the file, too.)

Share a File or Folder with Selected Users

You can also choose to share a file or folder with users you select. You can opt to let users only view or fully edit the given item.

1. From within the Files app, click My Drive under Google Drive in the sidebar; then navigate to the file or folder you want to share.

2. Click to select the file or folder you want to share.

3. Click the More Actions button on the toolbar.

4. Click Share with Others to open that file.

5. By default, all your files are private, except for those you share with people you specify. To share the file with a person, enter his or her Google Account username or standard email address into the Enter Names or Email Address box.

6. To make this file editable by the people you select, pull down the list to the right of the text box and select Can Edit.

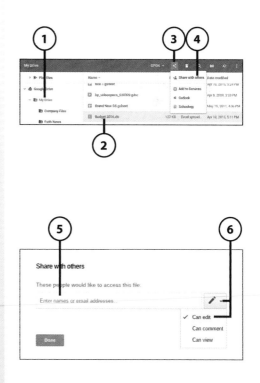

7. To allow viewers to enter comments about this file, pull down the list to the right of the text box and select Can Comment.

8. To make this file read-only (that is, no one else but you can edit it), pull down the list to the right of the text box and select Can View.

9. Click the Done button. The selected person has access to the file—and receives an email (including a link to the file) inviting him or her to view it online.

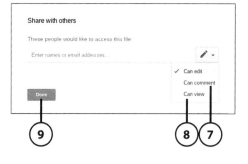

Share a Link to a File or Folder

Google Drive also lets you send a clickable link to anyone you want to share the file with. You can copy and paste this link into email messages, Facebook posts, web pages, and the like.

1. From within the Files app, click My Drive under Google Drive in the sidebar; then navigate to the file or folder you want to share.

2. Click to select the file or folder you want to share.

3. Click the More Actions button on the toolbar.

4. Click Share with Others.

5. Click Advanced to display the Sharing Settings pane.

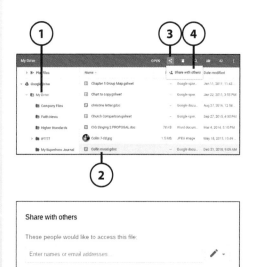

6. By default, your Google Drive files and folders are not sharable in this fashion, so you need to change this setting. In the Who Has Access section, where it says Private, click Change.

7. When the Link Sharing pane appears, select On – Anyone with the Link.

8. In the Access: Anyone (No Sign-In Required) section, click the down arrow and select whether you want users to view (Can View), comment on (Can Comment), or edit (Can Edit) the item.

9. Click Save.

10. The link to this file or folder is displayed and highlighted. Right-click the link (tap with two fingers once on the touchpad) and select Copy. (You can also opt to share directly via Gmail, Facebook, or Twitter.)

11. Click Cancel to close the panel and then paste the link into the message, document, or post to send to other users (not shown).

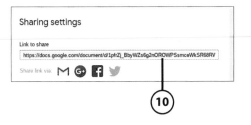

Sharing settings

Link to share (only accessible by collaborators)

ment/d/1pfrZj_BbyWZs6g2nOROWPSsmceWkSR68RWLj6-apDYQ/edit?usp=sharing

Share link via: M G+ f y

Who has access

Private - Only you can access   Change

Michael Miller (you)
molehillgroup@gmail.com

Edit the list of people who would like access and click Send.

Invite people:

⑥

⑦   **⑧**

Link sharing

On - Public on the web
Anyone on the Internet can find and access. No sign-in required.

On - Anyone with the link
Anyone who has the link can access. No sign-in required.

Off - Specific people
Shared with specific people.

Access: Anyone (no sign-in required)   Can view ▾

Note: Items with any link sharing option ca...   he web. Learn more

                                                                  Can edit

Save   Cancel   Can comment

                                                          ✓   Can view   ...about link sharing

⑨

Sharing settings

Link to share

https://docs.google.com/document/d/1pfrZj_BbyWZs6g2nOROWPSsmceWkSR68RV

Share link via: M G+ f y

⑩

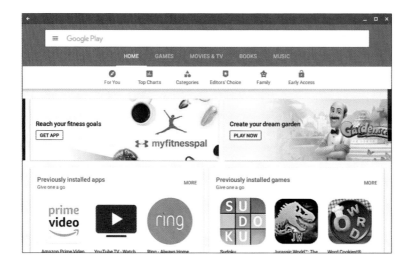

In this chapter, you learn how to add functionality to your Chromebook with fun and productive apps.

→ Understanding Chromebook Apps

→ Getting to Know the Google Play Store

→ Installing and Launching Apps

→ Managing Installed Apps

Using Chrome and Android Apps

If you have an iPhone or Android phone, you're used to the concept of apps—small, single-purpose applications that you run with the touch of a button. Well, apps also are available for your Chromebook, and you can use the Google Play Store to find the apps you want. There are many apps designed specifically for the Chrome OS (and Chrome browser)—plus your Chromebook can run apps designed for Google's Android mobile operating system.

Understanding Chromebook Apps

There are two types of apps that you can run on your Chromebook—Chrome apps and Android apps. They both work in similar fashion.

How Chrome Apps Work

A Chrome app is an application that you run in the Google Chrome browser. These apps, which can run either within the Chrome browser or in separate app windows, are actually web-based applications. This means that very little (if any) of the app code resides on your Chromebook; the bulk of the app is online (in the cloud) and thus requires an Internet connection to run.

For example, the app called Google Calendar is a web-based calendar and scheduling application. You access the app from Google Chrome, and it looks and acts like a regular application, but the app itself is hosted on Google's website, as is all your personal calendar and appointment data.

That said, some Chrome apps can run when you're not connected to the Internet. These are typically small, self-contained apps, such as the Calculator app, that don't need any cloud-based data to run.

Google ensures that Chrome apps look and act like the apps on your smartphone. They are always available to you, no matter what computer you're using. Find an app you like and you can run it on your Chromebook as well as within the Chrome browser on a Windows or Mac PC.

Here's something else: Apps are always up to date. When you run an app, you're running the current version offered by that website. No time-consuming (or costly) updates or upgrades are necessary.

On your Chromebook, you easily access your apps by clicking the Launcher icon on the Shelf. This displays the App Drawer; click the up arrow to expand the Drawer to full screen and see all the apps installed on your Chromebook. Click the little dots on the right side of the screen to display multiple pages of apps, or use the Search box to search for a specific app. Click any app to launch it.

You can find all manner of Chrome apps in the Google Play Store, which I discuss later in this chapter.

How Android Apps Work on Your Chromebook

In addition to apps developed specifically for Chrome OS, most newer Chromebooks also can run apps developed for Google's Android mobile operating system. These are the same apps you run on an Android mobile phone. So if you have an app you like on your Android phone, you also can run it on your Chromebook.

For all practical purposes, Android apps look and perform just like native Chrome apps. You won't be able to tell the difference, either in the Google

Play Store or when they're running on your Chromebook. You just have tons more apps available than you would with just Chrome-based apps. That's a good thing.

Note that not all Chromebooks support Android apps. In particular, this functionality is not available on older Chromebooks. If you're using a Chromebook manufactured since 2017, however, it's guaranteed to run Android apps with no problems. (If your Chromebook doesn't support Android functionality, you simply won't see those apps when you visit the Google Play Store.)

>>>Go Further

WHAT KINDS OF APPS ARE AVAILABLE?

What kinds of apps are available for your Chromebook? The list is long, and includes apps for both entertainment and productivity. The Google Play Store organizes apps into more than two dozen categories. And that's not even counting all the Chrome-based games that are available.

You can find apps for

- Productivity, such as Google Docs, Sheets, and Slides
- Social media, such as Facebook, Pinterest, and Twitter
- Movies and TV, such as Hulu, Netflix, and YouTube
- Music, such as Pandora and Spotify
- Photo editing, such as Adobe Photoshop Express and Google Photos

And that's just the tip of the iceberg. A surprisingly large number of these apps are available for free in the Google Play Store; some you'll have to pay for.

Getting to Know the Google Play Store

The Google Play Store is an online marketplace, hosted by Google, where you can browse and download thousands of different apps, games, and utilities for your Chromebook (and other devices running Chrome OS and Android). To visit the Google Play Store, open the Play Store app in the App Drawer.

Some of the items in the Google Play Store are developed by Google, others by various third-party developers. You can browse for items by category, or search for items using the top-of-page search box. Each item in the Google Play Store has its own information page, where you can read more about the item, contribute your own rating and review, and download the item to your Chromebook.

Most of the apps in the Google Play Store are free, but some cost money to download. Other apps may be free to download, but support in-app payments; that is, you may have to pay more in the future to continue using the app, or to activate enhanced functionality.

Installing and Launching Apps

As previously noted, you can find a huge number and variety of Chrome apps in the Google Play Store. Just click the Play Store icon in the App Drawer.

Download and Install an App

Apps are organized in the Google Play Store by category. You also can view best-selling apps, Editor's Choice apps, and apps recommended just for you.

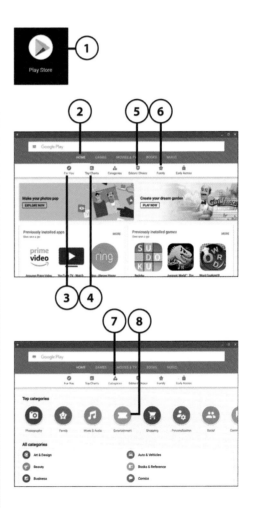

1. Open the App Drawer and click the Play Store icon.

2. The Home tab opens by default. Click another tab to view other types of items—games, videos (Movies & TV), books, and music.

3. Click For You to view recommended apps and games.

4. Click Top Charts to view the best-selling apps and games.

5. Click Editor's Choice to view apps and games handpicked by the Play Store editors.

6. Click Family to view apps and games specifically for kids and other family members.

7. Click Categories to display a list of categories.

8. Click a category to view apps within that chosen category.

9. Click an app icon to learn more about that app. The page for the selected app opens.

10. Click Reviews to read what other users say about this app.

11. Click Install to use this app.

12. The installation begins. When the installation is complete, click Open to begin using the app.

⑨   ⑩   ⑪

Pluto TV - It's Free TV
Pluto, Inc.

⑫

Launch an App

After you install a Chrome app, it appears in the App Drawer.

1. Click the Launcher icon on the Shelf to open the App Drawer.

2. Click the up arrow to expand the App Drawer.

3. Click the icon for the app you want to open.

②

①

③

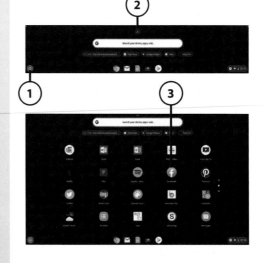

Using Chrome and Android Apps

Like traditional desktop applications, every Chrome or Android app is different and works in its own unique fashion. Creating a document in Google Docs, for example, is much different from reading posts in Twitter or playing Minecraft. You'll need to get to know each app you install to learn how to use it properly.

Managing Installed Apps

Chrome makes it easy to manage the apps you've installed—and configure how they launch.

Determine How an App Launches

By default, most Chrome apps open in a regular tab in the Chrome browser. You can open some apps, however, in a separate app window. (Not all apps have this option.)

1. From within the App Drawer, right-click the icon (tap with two fingers once on the touchpad) for the app you want to configure.

2. Select New Tab (or New Window, whichever is currently selected). If an app does not have this option, you don't see this menu item.

3. Select New Tab to open the app in a browser tab. *Or...*

4. Select New Window to open the app in a separate app window.

An app in a browser tab

An app in its own window

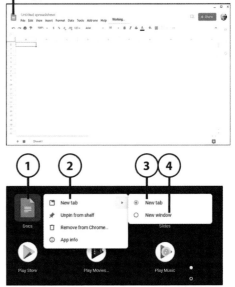

Uninstall an App

If you find you're not using a given app, you can remove the link to that app in your Chromebook.

1. From within the App Drawer, right-click the icon (tap with two fingers once on the touchpad) for the app you want to remove.

2. Select Uninstall or Remove from Chrome.

3. When prompted to remove the app, click Uninstall or Remove.

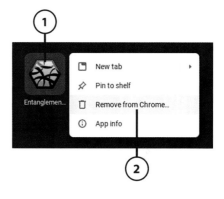

In this chapter, you learn how to use Google Cloud Print to print documents from your Chromebook.

→ Understanding Google Cloud Print
→ Connecting a Printer to Google Cloud Print
→ Printing to Google Cloud Print

Printing with Google Cloud Print

Printing from Chrome OS is substantially different than printing from Microsoft Windows or the Mac OS. It's more like printing from a tablet or mobile phone—you can't. At least not directly.

That's because like Android and iOS, Chrome OS doesn't have a native printing function. Instead, it uses a separate service, called Google Cloud Print, to print over the Internet to supported printers.

This means that your printing choices are a little different from what you're used to, in that you need a printer that's compatible with Google Cloud Print, or access to a normal printer connected to a Windows or Mac PC. Once everything's set up, however, printing is as simple as clicking a "print" button—only the setup is different.

Understanding Google Cloud Print

One of the things that makes Chrome OS different from other computer operating systems is that it doesn't carry with it a lot of legacy overhead—that is, the need to support older devices. That's one of the problems with Windows, for example; a large amount of programming code, disk space, and memory space is used to support thousands of printers and other devices from years past.

Google doesn't have that problem with Chrome OS; as a relatively new operating system, there are no older devices to support. And Google takes this approach even further by choosing not to directly support any of the current printers available today—at least not in the way that Windows or Mac OS do.

Instead, Google has embraced a technology dubbed Google Cloud Print. With this technology, Chrome is compatible with just a single device driver that is associated with the Cloud Print service. It's this service that then connects to various printers, reducing the load on the operating system.

The way Google Cloud Print works is simple. When you launch the "print" function in Chrome, the OS sends the print command over the Internet to the designated Cloud Print printer. The printer isn't physically connected to your Chromebook; the entire process is web-based.

Most new printers sold today support the Google Cloud Print technology. But what do you do if you have an older printer without built-in Cloud Print capability? Here, Google relies on other computers in your household or business. Cloud Print can print to any existing printer, as long as it's connected to a Windows or Mac computer that has Internet access. That is, Cloud Print relies on the computer for the connection—which means you have to have a Windows or Mac computer handy (and powered up).

The nice thing about Google Cloud Print is that you can use it to print from just about any device. Yes, you can print from your Chromebook to a Cloud Print printer, but you also can print from your iPhone or Android smartphone, your tablet, as well as from a Windows or Mac computer. And you can print from any location to any configured Cloud Print printer—which means you can be sitting in a hotel room in New York City and print to your Cloud Print printer back home in Omaha. No cables or printer drivers are necessary.

Connecting a Printer to Google Cloud Print

Before you can print from Google Chrome, you first must connect your printer to the Google Cloud Print service. You can connect either Cloud Print–ready printers or existing printers connected to a Windows or Mac computer.

Connect a Cloud Print–Ready Computer

If you're looking for a Cloud Print–ready printer, models are available from all major manufacturers. To use one of these printers for cloud printing, you must register it with the Google Cloud Print service. Follow your manufacturer's instructions to do so. (It's typically as simple as going to an online registration page and entering your printer's assigned email address.)

Connect an Older Printer

To connect an older printer to the Google Cloud Print service, it must be connected to a Windows or Mac computer that is connected to the Internet. The computer also must be running the Google Chrome web browser. You then enable the Google Cloud Print Connector, which connects this computer's printers to the Cloud Print service.

1. On your Windows or Mac computer, open the Google Chrome browser and, if necessary, sign in to your Google Account. Click the Customize and Control button to display the drop-down menu.

2. Click Settings.

3. Scroll to the bottom of the Settings page, click Advanced, and then go to the Printing section and click Google Cloud Print.

4. On the Google Cloud Print page, click Manage Cloud Print Devices.

5. In the Classic Printers section, click the Add Printers. (Any printers already set up are listed on the bottom of this page.)

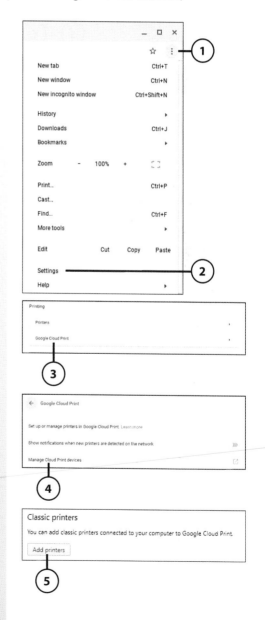

6. You now see all printers connected either directly or indirectly (over your home network) to this computer. Check those printers you want to add to the Cloud Print service.

7. Click the Add Printer(s) button to add the selected printers to the Cloud Print service.

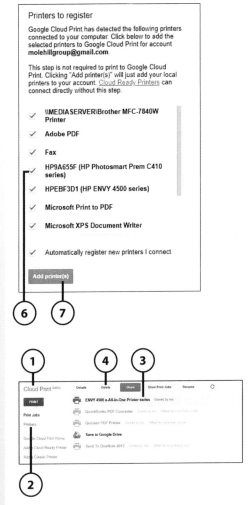

Disconnect a Printer from Cloud Print

You can remove a printer from the Google Cloud Print service.

1. From within Chrome, go to https://www.google.com/cloudprint/manage.html.

2. Click the Printers tab on the left.

3. Click the printer you want to disconnect.

4. Click the Delete button, and then click OK.

Printing to Google Cloud Print

Once you've registered a printer with the Google Cloud Print service, printing from your Chromebook is as easy as clicking a button. In fact, you can print from any computer, smartphone, or other device to that printer; all you need to do is provide your Google Account information.

Print from Your Chromebook

To print from your Chromebook to a printer connected to Google Cloud Print, that printer must be powered on and connected to the Internet. If it's a "classic" printer, it also must be connected to a Windows or Mac PC that is connected to the Internet.

1. From within Chrome, open the web page or application document you want to print (not shown).

2. Press Ctrl+P, or click the Customize and Control button and select Print.

3. When the Print panel appears, select the printer you want to use in the Destination section.

4. To print more than one copy, enter a number into the Copies box.

5. Click the Print button.

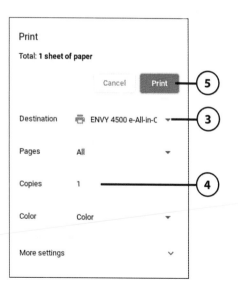

In this chapter, you learn how to keep in touch with friends, family, and colleagues via Messages for Web and Google Duo.

→ Sending and Receiving Texts with Messages for Web
→ Video Calling with Google Duo

13

Texting and Video Calling

You know that you can send and receive email with your Chromebook. (And I talk about that in the next chapter.) But did you know you also can send and receive text messages on your Chromebook? Or chat with friends and family via video?

Well, you can, with the right apps. You use Messages for Web for text messaging and Google Duo for video calls. Both of these apps are available for free from the Google Play Store.

Sending and Receiving Texts with Messages for Web

If you're like me, you do most of your "talking" to friends, family, and business associates via text messages on your mobile phone. When you're anchored to your desk, however, it might be easier to send and receive texts from your Chromebook, with its bigger and easier-to-use real keyboard.

If you're using an Android phone with Google's Messages texting app, you can do just that. The Google Messages for Web app installs on your Chromebook and links to your Android phone. Messages for Web lets you receive on your Chromebook all the texts that come to your phone, as well as send new texts directly from your Chromebook. It's a snap.

Configure Messages for Web

You download and install the Messages for Web app for free from the Google Play Store. You then need to configure it to work with your Android phone and the Messages phone app. To do this, you need both your Chromebook and your phone.

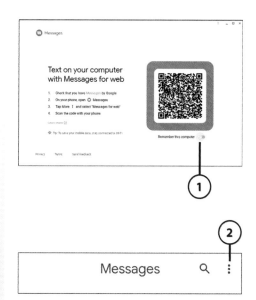

1. On your Chromebook, open the Messages for Web app. Switch "on" the Remember This Computer switch.

2. On your phone, open to the Messages app. From the main screen, tap the More (three-dot) icon.

3. Tap Messages for Web.

4. Tap QR Code Scanner.

5. Aim your phone's camera at the QR code in the Chromebook app.

That's it. The Messages for Web app on your Chromebook should link to the Messages app on your phone and display a list of your recent text conversations.

It's Not All Good

Android Only

The only downside to the Messages for Web app is that it works only with Android phones, not iPhones. Your phone also has to be using Google's Messages app, not another texting app.

So, for example, if you use an iPhone, you can't use Messages for Web. Likewise, if you have an Android phone with a different texting app, such as those that AT&T and other carriers offer, you have to switch to Google's Messages app before you can use Messages to Web.

Resume a Text Chat

The Messages for Web app automatically imports your contact list and all
recent text conversations. It's easy to
resume a previous conversation.

1.   When you launch Messages for
     Web, all your previous chats are
     listed in the left panel. Click a chat
     to view your previous message
     exchanges in the main pane.

2.   Your texts appear on the right
     side of the main panel. The per-
     son or group of people you're
     texting with appear on the left.

3.   Enter a message into the Text
     Message field.

4.   Click the SMS button to send the
     text.

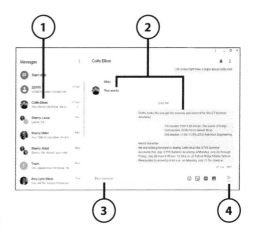

Pictures and Other Attachments

Just as with the phone-based Messages
app, Messages for Web lets you attach
pictures and other files to your text
messages. Click the Select Attachment
icon on the far right of the Text Message
field; then navigate to and select the
image or other file you want to send.

Start a New Text Chat

It's equally easy to send a new text
message.

1.   Click Start Chat.

2.   Click one of your top contacts to
     text that person. *Or…*

3.   Enter a contact's name, phone
     number, or email address into the
     To: field.

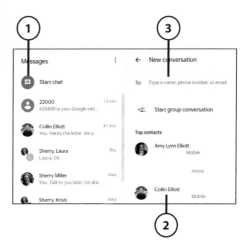

4. As you type, matching contacts are listed. Select a contact's name from the list.

5. Enter a message into the Text Message field.

6. Click the SMS button to send the text.

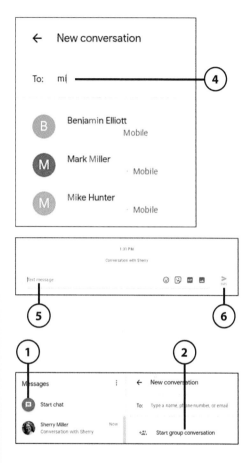

Start a Group Conversation

Just as you can text a group of people on your phone, you can use Messages for Web to participate in group texts on your Chromebook.

1. Click Start Chat.

2. Click Start Group Conversation.

3. Enter the first person's contact's name, phone number, or email address into the To: field.

4. Select the person's name from the list.

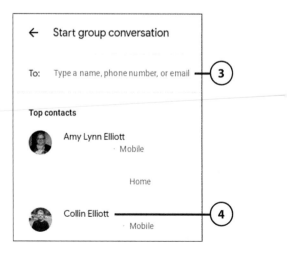

5. Click Add More People and repeat steps 3 and 4 to add more people to the conversation.

6. Click Next when you're done adding people.

7. Enter a message into the Text Message field.

8. Click the MMS button to send the text.

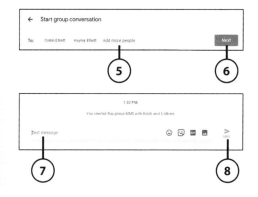

Video Calling with Google Duo

Sometimes what you really want is a face-to-face conversation with a friend or family member. But what do you do when you're not together to talk?

The solution is to make a video call. All you need is your Chromebook (with its built-in webcam, microphone, and speakers), an Internet connection, and the Google Duo app. (Of course, the person you want to chat with also needs the Google Duo app installed on her device.)

Duo-Compatible Devices

Versions of the Google Duo app are available for Chromebooks, Windows and Mac computers, and Android and iOS phones and tablets. You can download the Chrome version of Duo (for free) from the Google Play Store.

Start a Call

When you first launch the Google Duo app, you're prompted to give access to your microphone, camera, and contacts; click Give Access. Then you are prompted to allow or deny Duo to access your contacts; click Agree to accept their policies.

You're prompted to enter your phone number; this is how the app identifies you and enables you to chat with your contacts. Click Agree. (At this point, you may receive a text on your phone with a verification number. If so, enter this number into Duo.)

Once everything is set up (which literally takes just seconds), you're ready to start calling friends and family.

1. In the left panel, make sure the Video Call Mode is selected.

2. Select one of the contacts displayed. *Or...*

3. Enter a person's name or phone number into the Search Contacts box, and then select the person you want.

4. Duo dials the other person. When he answers, you see his picture in the main window and a small thumbnail of you in the corner. Start talking!

5. Click End Call to end the video call.

Voice Calls

Google Duo also lets you engage in voice calls with your contacts. Select Voice Call Mode from the left column of the main screen and then start a new call as usual.

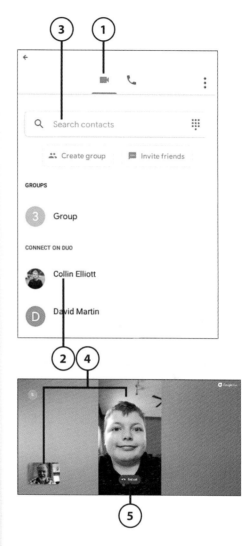

Manage a Group Call

Google Duo also lets you create group video and voice calls. This is great for larger family get-togethers or school or business meetings.

1. From the main screen, select either Video Call Mode or Voice Call Mode, and then click Create Group.

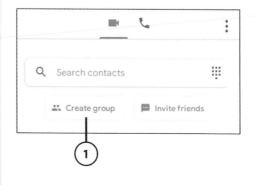

2. Search or browse for contacts, and then click to select those you want in the group chat.

3. Click Done.

4. Click the Start button. Group members receive notifications to join the group call.

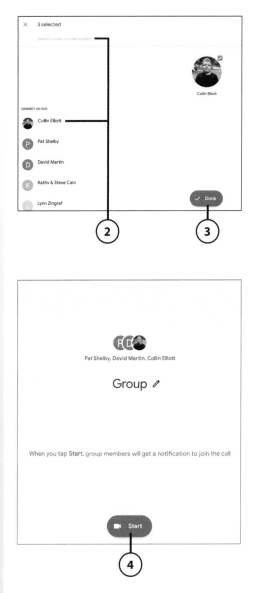

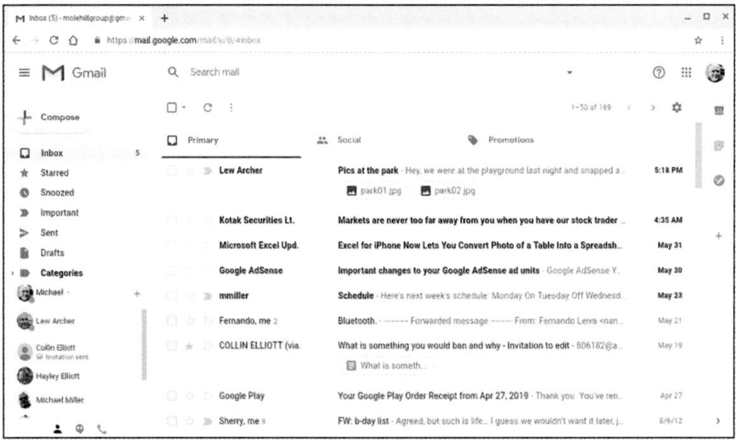
Inbox (5) - molehillgroup@gm
https://mail.google.com/mail/u/0/#inbox
Gmail
Search mail
Compose
Inbox 5
Starred
Snoozed
Important
Sent
Drafts
Categories
Michael
Lew Archer
Collin Elliott
Hayley Elliott
Michael Miller
1–50 of 189
Primary
Social
Promotions
Lew Archer
Pics at the park - Hey, we were at the playground last night and snapped a...
5:18 PM
park01.jpg
park02.jpg
Kotak Securities Lt.
Markets are never too far away from you when you have our stock trader ...
4:35 AM
Microsoft Excel Upd.
Excel for iPhone Now Lets You Convert Photo of a Table Into a Spreadsh...
May 31
Google AdSense
Important changes to your Google AdSense ad units - Google AdSense Y...
May 30
mmiller
Schedule - Here's next week's schedule: Monday On Tuesday Off Wednesd...
May 23
Fernando, me 2
Bluetooth. - ------- Forwarded message ------ From: Fernando Leiva
May 21
COLLIN ELLIOTT (via
What is something you would ban and why - Invitation to edit - 806182@a...
May 19
What is someth...
Google Play
Your Google Play Order Receipt from Apr 27, 2019 - Thank you. You've ren...
Apr 27
Sherry, me 9
FW: b-day list - Agreed, but such is life... I guess we wouldn't want it later, j...
8/6/12

In this chapter, you learn how to send and receive email with Google's Gmail service.

→ Reading and Replying to Messages
→ Sending New Messages
→ Managing Your Messages

14

Emailing with Gmail

Gmail is the largest email service today. Not surprisingly, you can use Gmail on your Chromebook to send and receive email messages. The Gmail app is already installed when you first power up your Chromebook; in fact, you use your Google Account and your Gmail address to log in to your Chromebook.

Reading and Replying to Messages

The Gmail app opens in its own tab in the Chrome browser. The navigation pane on the left includes links to your Gmail Inbox and other important folders, as well as your most-used contacts. The contents of the selected folder are displayed in the main pane.

When Gmail launches, the Inbox, which contains all your received messages, is selected by default. You can view other folders by clicking them in the navigation pane. For example, to view all your sent mail, simply scroll down the folder list and click Sent.

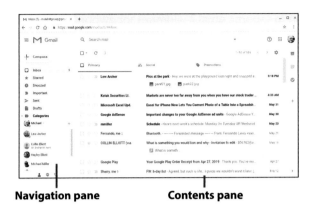

Navigation pane **Contents pane**

Gmail attempts, though not always successfully, to organize your incoming mail by type and display each type of message on a separate tab in the contents pane. The Primary tab displays standard correspondence; the Social tab displays messages from Facebook and other social networks; and the Promotions tab displays advertising email. Click a tab to read all messages of a given type.

Read Messages

Within the Inbox, each message is listed with the message's sender, the message's subject, a snippet from the message, and the date or time the message was sent. (The snippet typically is the first line of the message text.)

Unread inbox messages are listed in bold; after a message has been read, it's displayed in normal, nonbold text with a shaded background. And if you've assigned a label to a message (discussed later in this chapter), the label appears before the message subject.

Group Actions

To perform an action on a message or group of messages in the Inbox, such as deleting them, put a check mark by the message(s), and then click one of the buttons at the top of the list. Alternatively, you can click the More button to display a list of additional actions to perform.

1. Click to open the Inbox.

2. Click the tab for the type of message you want to view. (Most of your important messages will be on the Primary tab.)

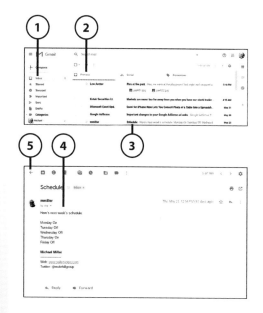

3. Click the header for the message you want to view.

4. You see the contents of the selected message.

5. To return to the Inbox, click the Back to Inbox button.

View Conversations

One of the unique things about Gmail is that all related email messages are grouped in what Google calls *conversations*. A conversation might be an initial message and all its replies (and replies to replies). A conversation also might be all the daily emails from a single source with a common subject, such as messages you receive from subscribed-to mailing lists.

A conversation is noted in the inbox list by a number in parentheses after the sender name(s). If a conversation has replies from more than one person, more than one name is listed.

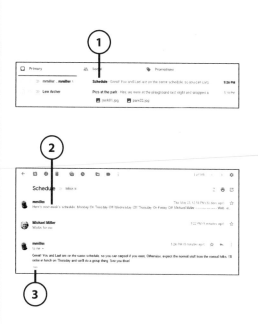

1. To view a conversation, simply click the message title. The most recent message displays in full.

2. To view the text of any longer individual message in a conversation, click that message's header.

3. To expand *all* the messages in a conversation, click the Expand All link. All the messages in the conversation are stacked on top of each other, with the text of the newest message fully displayed.

View Pictures and Other Attachments

Many people use email to send pictures and other files to their friends, family, and colleagues. These files are attached to an email message and are called *attachments*. If a message has a file attached, you'll see a paper clip icon next to the message in the Inbox.

1. When viewing a message, you see any attached photos as thumbnail images. Click a thumbnail to view the picture full size in Chrome's photo viewer.

2. Mouse over an attached folder or file and then click the Download icon to download it to your Chromebook.

3. Mouse over an item and then click the Save to Drive icon to save an attached file to Google Drive.

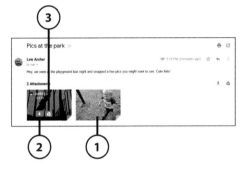

Reply to Messages

Whether you're reading a single message or a conversation, it's easy to reply to that message.

1. In the original message, click the Reply button to expand the message to include a reply box.

2. The original sender is automatically added as the new recipient. Add your new text into the reply box.

3. To send the message, click the Send button.

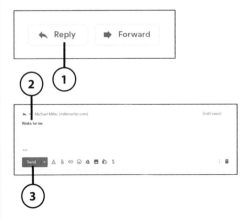

Reply to All

If a conversation has multiple participants, you can reply to all of them by clicking the down arrow next to the Reply button and then selecting Reply to All.

Forward Messages

You also can forward an existing message to another party.

1. In the original message, click the
   Forward button. This expands the
   message to include a forward box.

2. Add the recipient's email address
   in the To box.

3. Enter your message into the main
   message box.

4. Click the Send button to send the
   message.

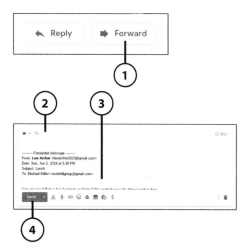

Sending New Messages

It's easy to compose and send new messages with Gmail. When you need to,
you can attach one or more files to a message. You also can add a signature
to your messages.

Compose a New Message

New messages you send are composed in
a New Message pane that appears at the
bottom-right corner of the Gmail window.

1. Click the Compose button at the
   top of the left column on any
   Gmail page. This opens a New
   Message pane.

2. Enter the recipient's email address
   in the To box. Gmail will suggest
   recipients from your contacts list;
   choose one of these suggestions
   or continue typing the address.
   Separate multiple recipients with
   commas.

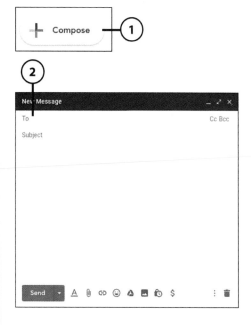

3. Enter a subject for the message into the Subject box.

4. Enter the text of your message in the large text box. Click any of the options in the Formatting toolbar at the bottom of the pane to enhance your text with bold, italic, and other formats.

5. Click the Send button when you're done composing your message.

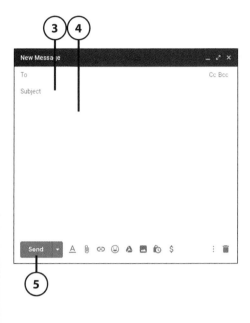

Spell Checking

Gmail includes a built-in spell checker. Any potentially misspelled words are identified with a squiggly red underline. Right-click a word (tap two fingers once on the touchpad) to see a list of suggested spellings; click the correct spelling to fix the word.

>>>Go Further
CC AND BCC

You can also carbon copy and blind carbon copy additional recipients to a message. With a carbon copy (Cc), the original recipients see the new recipient. With a blind carbon copy (Bcc), the new recipient's name is hidden from the original recipients.

To add a Cc or Bcc, click either the Cc or Bcc link in the New Message pane. This expands the message to include a Cc or Bcc box, into which you enter the recipients' email addresses.

Attach a File to a Message

When you need to send a digital photo or some other file to a friend or colleague, you can do so via email. To send a file via email, you attach that file to a standard email message. When the message is sent, the file attachment travels along with it; when the message is received, the file is right there, waiting to be opened.

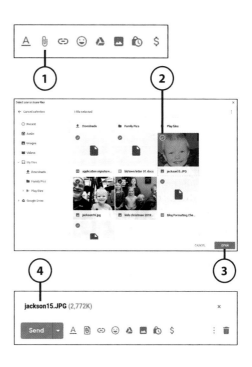

1. Compose a new message and then click the Attach Files (paper clip) button at the bottom of the New Message pane.

2. When the Files app opens, navigate to and select the file you want to attach.

3. Click the Open button.

4. The file you selected appears at the bottom of the New Message pane. Continue to compose your message, and then send it as normal.

Add a Signature to Your Messages

A *signature* is personalized text that appears at the bottom of an email message. Signatures typically include the sender's name and contact information, or some personal message. Gmail lets you create a single signature and apply it to all your outgoing email messages.

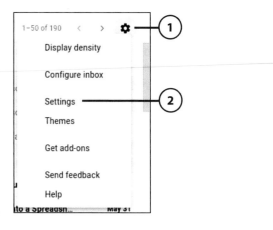

1. Click the Settings button.

2. Click Settings to display the Gmail Settings page with the General tab selected.

3. Scroll down to the Signature section and enter your desired signature into the text box. This deselects the No Signature option.

4. Use the formatting controls to format your signature.

5. Click the Insert This Signature Before Quoted Text in Replies option if you want to include your signature in the replies you make to email messages.

6. Scroll to the bottom of the page and click the Save Changes button. Your signature will be automatically added to all new email messages you compose.

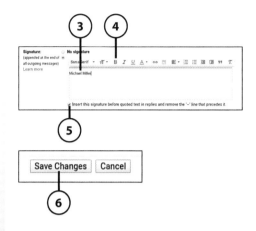

Managing Your Messages

When you receive a lot of messages in your Inbox, the sheer number can become unwieldy. Fortunately, Gmail offers several ways to manage the messages you receive.

Assign Labels to a Message

Unlike other services, Gmail doesn't let you organize messages into folders. Instead, Gmail lets you "tag" messages with one or more labels. This has the effect of creating virtual folders, as you can search and sort your messages by any of the labels you create.

1. In the Gmail Inbox, check those messages you want to share the same label.

2. Click the Labels button. Gmail displays a list of all existing labels.

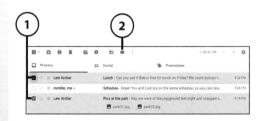

3. Select a label from the list. *Or…*

4. Select Create New from the list to create a new label. The New Label dialog box opens.

5. Enter the name of the new label.

6. Click the Create button. Now the label you just created is added to the navigation pane. The messages you checked will appear when you click this newly created label.

Multiple Labels

You can apply multiple labels to a single message. To apply another label to the same message(s), just repeat this procedure. After you assign a label, that label appears before the message's subject line.

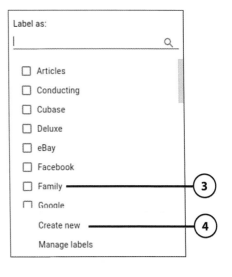

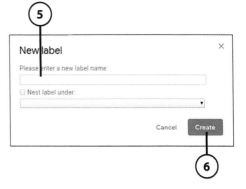

Filter Messages by Label

After you've assigned labels to your messages, all of these labels appear in the Labels list, which appears beneath your folders in the navigation pane. You can use this list to display only those messages that have a specific label.

1. In the Gmail Inbox, scroll to the Labels list in the navigation pane and click the desired label.

2. Gmail displays all the messages designated with that label.

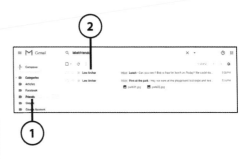

Search for Messages

You can also search your Gmail Inbox for messages that contain specific text or that are from a specific sender.

1. Enter your search query, in the form of one or more keywords, into the Search box at the top of any Gmail page; then press Enter.

2. Gmail returns a search results page. This page lists messages in which the keywords you entered appear anywhere in the email—in the subject line, in the message text, or in the sender or recipient lists. Click a message to read it.

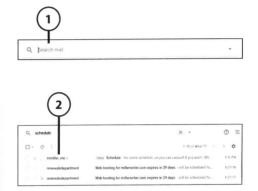

Delete Messages

You can easily delete one or more messages from the Inbox.

1. From the Gmail Inbox, check those messages you want to delete.

2. Click the Delete button.

In this chapter, you learn how to view movies, TV shows, and other videos on your Chromebook.

→ Watching Netflix and Other Streaming Video Services
→ Watching Local TV Stations and Cable Networks
→ Watching Videos on YouTube

Watching Streaming Video

Many television viewers are "cutting the cord" by disconnecting from cable service and instead watching their favorite programs online on their computers. Not surprisingly, it's easy to use your Chromebook to watch television shows and movies online, via Netflix, Hulu, and other streaming video services.

Watching Netflix and Other Streaming Video Services

There's a ton of programming on the Web that you don't have to purchase or download as large video files. This programming is available via a technology called *streaming video*, which is perfect for viewing on your Chromebook. It works by streaming the movie or TV show you pick over the Internet in real time to your Chromebook; then you watch the programming in the Chrome browser. You can find tens of thousands of free and paid videos to watch from dozens of streaming video services.

You access all the streaming video services discussed in this chapter via their own Chrome or Android apps, which are downloadable (for free) from the Google Play Store. Just download and install an app, and then click the app icon to launch the streaming video service on your Chromebook. Some services are free; most require a monthly subscription fee.

The three most popular streaming video services, all with Chromebook apps, are Amazon Prime Video, Hulu, and Netflix. Each offers some sort of free trial period, so you can try them out before you commit.

Watching Amazon Prime Video

Amazon Prime Video is an extension of Amazon's Prime service, which gives you free two-day shipping on selected Amazon purchases. If you're a Prime member, your subscription to Amazon Prime Video is free.

The Amazon Prime Video app —

Amazon Prime Video offers a wide selection of new and older movies and TV series, although this selection is weighted toward newer movies and shows. There is also a lot of original programming, called Prime Originals; these programs include *Bosch*, *Forever*, *Good Omens*, *The Man in the High Castle*, *The Marvelous Mrs. Maisel*, *Tom Clancy's Jack Ryan*, *Sneaky Pete*, and *Transparent*. Amazon Prime Video also offers a variety of movies and TV shows for purchase or rental; once you've paid for an item, you can then stream it for viewing on your Chromebook.

Prime Subscriptions
The Amazon Prime shipping membership costs $119 USD per year, and includes Amazon Prime Video. If you're not a Prime member, you can subscribe to only Prime Video for $8.99 USD per month. Given the minimal difference in price, most people are better off getting the whole Prime membership (with Prime Video thrown in free) than paying for Prime Video separately.

Watching Hulu

Like Amazon Prime Video, Hulu is a subscription service that offers free streaming of movies, TV series, and original programming. Hulu was originally conceived as a place to watch recent episodes of current TV series—kind of a "catch-up" service. It still offers access to recent TV shows but has added all manner of other content, including older TV series, movies, and original programming.

The Hulu app

In terms of original programming, Hulu is starting to make a name for itself. You'll find a number of well-regarded original series, including *Catch-22*, *Future Man*, *The Handmaid's Tale*, *Harlots*, and *Marvel's Runaways*.

Hulu offers two basic plans, with and (sort of) without commercials. What Hulu calls the Limited Commercials plan runs $5.99 USD per month and inserts commercials into the programs you watch. (And it's not really a limited number, either; some programs have a *lot* of commercials!) If you want to minimize the number of commercials you see, sign up for the $11.99 USD No Commercials plan—but know that you'll still see commercials on some programs—just fewer of them.

Watching Netflix

Netflix is the most popular streaming service today, with more than 137 million subscribers worldwide. Like Amazon Prime Video and Hulu, Netflix offers unlimited video streaming for a monthly subscription price. It started out offering mainly movies but has shifted over the years to add a variety of newer and classic TV shows, plus a plethora of original programming. It's a fairly well-rounded service.

The Netflix app

Netflix is the leader in original programming, both series and movies. Its original series are well known and well respected, and include *Black Mirror, Chilling Adventures of Sabrina, The Crown, Fuller House, GLOW, Grace and Frankie, House of Cards, Lost in Space, Orange Is the New Black, Russian Doll, Stranger Things*, and *The Umbrella Academy*.

Netflix offers three different subscription plans: Basic ($8.99/month), Standard ($12.99/month), and Premium ($15.99/month). The big difference is how many users can watch at the same time, from just 1 (Basic) to 2 (Standard) to 4 (Premium).

Watching Other Streaming Video Services

Amazon Prime Video, Hulu, and Netflix may be the largest streaming video services, but they're far from the only ones. There are dozens of other streaming video services available for viewing on your Chromebook. Table 15.1 details some of the more popular ones.

Table 15.1   Other Streaming Video Services

Service	Description	Monthly Subscription
Acorn TV	Programming from the UK, Canada, and New Zealand	$5.99
BritBox	UK programming from the BBC and ITV	$6.99
BroadwayHD	Broadway shows and concerts	$8.99
CBS All Access	CBS network and original programming, including *Star Trek Discovery, Star Trek Picard,* and *The Twilight Zone*	$5.99
Crackle Plus	Older movies and TV shows	Free
Criterion Channel	Classic films from the Criterion Collection	$10.99
DC Universe	DC superhero movies and TV shows, including original programming such as *Doom Patrol, Swamp Thing,* and *Teen Titans*	$7.99

Service	Description	Monthly Subscription
FilmRise	Movies, TV shows from the 1980s and '90s	Free
Popcornflix	Older movies, reality TV shows, children's programming	Free
Shout Factory TV	Classic and cult TV shows and movies (including *Mystery Science Theater 3000*)	Free
Showtime	Original Showtime programming	$10.99
Starz	Original programming from the Starz networks	$8.99
Tubi	Older movies and TV shows, reality TV shows	Free

New Streaming Services

There are new video streaming services being launched seemingly every week. In particular, be on the lookout for new services from Disney, NBC/Universal, and WarnerMedia coming later in 2019.

>>>Go Further

STREAMING VIDEO FROM YOUR CHROMEBOOK TO YOUR LIVING ROOM TV

Watching movies and TV shows on your Chromebook is fine when you're on the go, but it's not the same as watching programming on the big flat-screen TV you have in your living room. To that end, you can connect most Chromebooks to your living room TV, with a single cable.

If your Chromebook has an HDMI output (and most do), it's easy to connect an HDMI cable between your Chromebook and your living room TV. (HDMI is the cable technology used to connect high-definition Blu-ray players, cable boxes, and other equipment to flat-screen TVs; the HDMI cable carries both audio and video signals.) Once you have the cable connected, start the streaming video app on your Chromebook, as you would normally, and then switch your TV to the corresponding HDMI input. The programming you're playing on your Chromebook is now displayed on your TV. Sit back and start watching.

Watching Local TV Stations and Cable Networks

Hulu and other similar services are great for catching up on your favorite TV shows, but they don't let you watch those shows live in real time. In the past, if you wanted to watch TV shows live, you needed either an OTA (over-the-air) antenna (not always easy or practical) or a cable or satellite subscription (pricey). Now, however, there's another alternative: live TV streaming services.

A live streaming video service does just what the description implies—it lets you watch live TV, from both local channels and cable/satellite channels, over the Internet. This type of service displays a program guide, like the kind from a cable or satellite provider, with available channels listed by time of day. Channels are streamed in real time, as they're broadcast, for playback on your Chromebook or other device.

The program guide for YouTube TV

There are a number of live streaming video apps available for downloading from the Google Play Store. None of these services are free; all have a monthly subscription fee.

Local Stations

Most live streaming services offer a variety of local TV stations, but not always all the stations available in your area. If you live in a large metropolitan area, chances are most of your local stations will be available on most live streaming services, but it isn't guaranteed. There are many cities where one or more local stations simply aren't available on a given live streaming service. This is something you need to check for specifically before you sign up for a service.

Table 15.2 details the major live streaming services available for viewing on your Chromebook. A few things to note:

- Cable channel lineups and local station availability differ significantly from service to service. In general, the more expensive services offer more channels.

- Each service offers different subscription levels. Again, the more you pay, the more channels you get.

- While all these services have Chrome or Android apps, some services require you to view their programming from their website in the Chrome browser. Follow the onscreen instructions to proceed.

Table 15.2   Live Streaming Video Services

Service	Monthly Subscription
AT&T Watch TV	$15.00+
DirecTV Now	$50.00+
fuboTV	$54.99+
Hulu with Live TV	$44.99+
PlayStation Vue	$44.99+
Sling TV	$25.00+
YouTube TV	$50.00+

Hulu with Live TV and YouTube TV

Don't confuse the regular Hulu app with the Hulu with Live TV service; the latter offers full live streaming, complete with local and cable channels. Likewise, don't confuse YouTube with YouTube TV; again, the latter is the live streaming service.

Watching Videos on YouTube

There's one more streaming video service worth discussing, although it's not a direct competitor to Amazon Prime Video, Hulu, or Netflix. That service is YouTube, Google's video-sharing community, where its legion of users upload and view all manner of videos on all manner of devices.

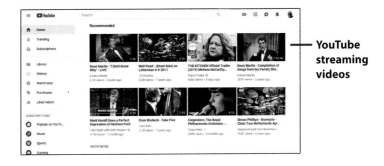

YouTube streaming videos

Anyone can upload a video to YouTube, and at times it seems like practically everyone has. There are tons of how-to and self-improvement videos on YouTube, as well as prank, funny animals and funny humans, videogame play-throughs, product reviews, you name it. There are also tons of old television programs uploaded by users, as well as old and new music videos, movie trailers, and the like. And, best of all, YouTube is all free—no monthly subscription required.

Your Chromebook should have come with the YouTube app already installed. If not, you can find it in the Google Play Store.

Spotify   Pandora   Play Music

16

Listening to Streaming Music

Many people like to listen to music on their Chromebooks. Maybe you like a little background music while you're browsing Facebook or working on a Google Docs document. Or maybe your Chromebook is your primary source of music, blasting your favorite tunes across the entire room. In any case, you can use your Chromebook to listen to millions of tunes streamed online from Spotify, Pandora, Google Play Music, and similar services.

How Streaming Music Services Work

It used to be that music lovers bought vinyl albums and singles. Sometime in the mid-1980s, they switched to buying digital compact discs. Then, at the turn of the century, there was another shift, to downloading digital music over the Internet.

Today, another shift is in progress. Instead of buying music one track or album at a time, more and more people are subscribing to online music services that let you listen to all the songs you want, either for free or a low monthly charge. These services, such as Pandora, Spotify, and Google Play Music, stream music in real time over the

Internet to your Chromebook; there's nothing to download, nothing to store on your computer, and it's all perfectly legal.

There are two primary types of delivery services for streaming audio online. The first model is like traditional radio in that you can't dial up specific tunes; you have to listen to whatever the service beams out, although it comes in the form of personalized playlists or virtual radio stations. The second model, typified by Spotify, lets you specify which songs you want to listen to; this type of service is called an *on-demand service*.

Some streaming audio services offer both types of delivery. Pandora, for example, offers a free service that plays personalized "stations" but doesn't include on-demand listening. Pandora also has a paid service that lets you dial up specific songs, albums, and artists. You can pick the type of streaming music service that best fits your needs.

Listening to Pandora

Pandora was one of the first and remains one of the most popular streaming music services. You can access Pandora from the Chrome browser at www. pandora.com or from the free Pandora app available in the Google Play Store. Pandora claims to have more than 40 million tracks in its music library.

Subscription Plans

Pandora offers three different subscription plans.

The basic plan is free, but you have to sign up and sign in. The free plan is much like traditional AM or FM radio, in that you listen to the songs Pandora selects for you, along with accompanying commercials. It's a little more personalized than traditional radio, however, in that you create personalized stations (up to 100). All you have to do is choose a song or artist; Pandora then creates a station with other songs like the one you picked. This plan is ad-supported, so you'll be subjected to commercials every handful of songs—just as with traditional radio.

Pandora Plus is just like the free plan, but it cuts out the commercials. For this, you pay $4.99 per month.

Pandora Premium, at $9.99 per month (or $14.99 per month for the Family plan, which includes up to six accounts), is a bit different. In addition to the personalized stations, you also get on-demand playback. That is, you can search for and play any song in the Pandora library. You also can create personalized playlists of songs you select.

Create a New Station

Central to all three plans is the ability to create personalized music stations. A station can be based on a specific song, artist, or genre. You specify what you like, and Pandora plays other songs that are similar.

1. From the home screen of the Pandora app, click the Search icon.

2. Enter the name of a song, genre, artist, or composer.

3. Pandora lists items that match your search. Click a tab to view only artists, songs, stations, podcasts, playlists, or albums.

4. Click the item you want.

5. If you selected an artist, click a specific song or radio station to listen to.

6. Click the Play button to play this particular item.

7. Click Start Station to create a station based on this item.

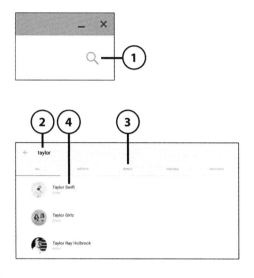

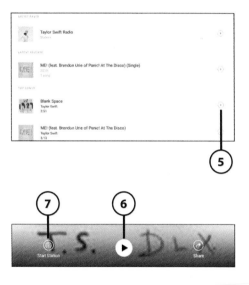

Play a Station

When you start playing a Pandora station, you can't go back. You can pause the current song or skip to the next song, but you can't repeat songs.

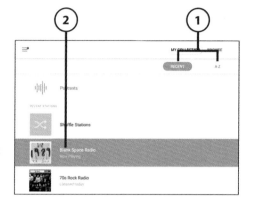

1. All your stations are listed on the Pandora home screen. Click Recent to view recently played stations, or click A–Z to view your entire list of stations in alphabetical order.

2. Click an item to begin playing that playlist.

3. Pause playback by clicking the Pause button. Click Play to resume playback.

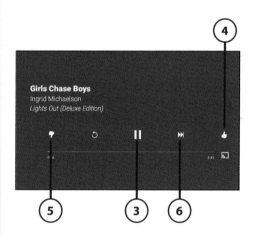

4. Click Thumbs-Up to "like" the current song. Pandora plays more songs like this one.

5. If you don't like the current song, click Thumbs-Down. Pandora skips to the next song, doesn't play the current song again, and plays fewer songs like it.

6. Click Next Track to skip to the next song without disliking it. (Note that with the free plan, you get a limited number of skips each session.)

>>>Go Further

LOCAL RADIO STATIONS ONLINE

If you'd rather just listen to your local AM or FM radio station—or to a radio station located in another city—you can do so over the Internet. There are several streaming services that offer access to radio stations around the world, including iHeartRadio, Radio.com, and TuneIn. All have free apps in the Google Play Store.

Listening to Spotify

Another big streaming music service is Spotify, which lets you choose specific tracks to listen to on demand and enables you to create personalized play-lists. Like Pandora, Spotify has more than 40 million songs in its online library.

Subscription Plans

Spotify's basic membership is free, but you're subjected to commercials every few songs. If you want to get rid of the commercials and get unlimited skips, sign up for the $9.99 per month Spotify Premium plan (or $14.99 per month for the Family plan, which includes up to six accounts).

Listen to Music

You can access Spotify from within the Chrome browser (www.spotify.com) or from the Spotify app, available from the Google Play Store. Listening to music on Spotify is as easy as searching for a song and then playing it.

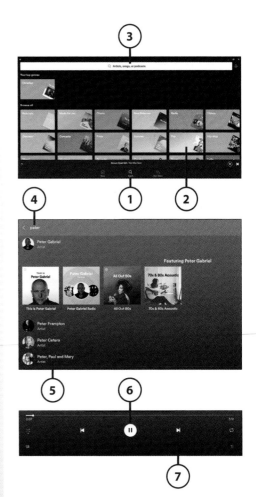

1. From within the Spotify app, click the Search icon.

2. Click one of the genre tiles to browse by that musical genre.

3. Click the Search box to search for a specific song, album, or artist.

4. Enter your query into the Search box. As you type, Spotify displays matching items.

5. Click the item you want to play.

6. Playback starts automatically. Click the Pause button to pause playback. Click Play to resume playback.

7. If you're playing a playlist or album, click the Next button to skip to the next track.

Listening to Google Play Music

Google also has a streaming music service, called Google Play Music. Like Pandora and Spotify, it offers more than 40 million tracks for streaming online. The Google Play Music app is preinstalled on all new Chromebooks.

Subscription Plans

Google Play Music offers two subscription music plans. The free plan is like Pandora's free plan; you get personalized "radio" stations interrupted by occasional commercials. The Unlimited plan, at $9.99 per month (or $14.99 for the Family plan, which includes up to six accounts), adds the ability to play any individual song on demand.

Listen to Music

If you've signed up for Google Play Music's free plan, you can search for and play "radio" stations that fit your musical mood.

1. From within the Google Play Music app, click within the top-of-page Search box.

2. Enter the song, artist, album, or genre you want. As you type, Google suggests matching items.

3. Click the one you want, or continue entering your search and press Enter.

4. Click the Play button to start playback.

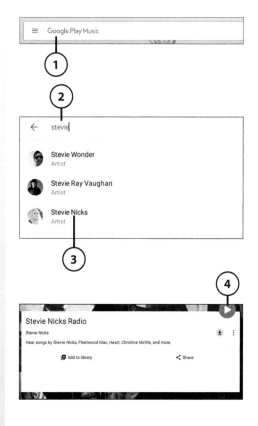

5. You see playback controls at the bottom of the main window. Click Pause to pause playback. Click Play to resume playback.

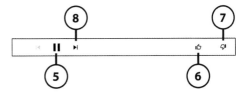

6. Click Thumbs-Up to like this track and play more like it.

7. Click Thumbs-Down to play fewer songs like this one.

8. Click Next to skip to the next track.

In this chapter, you learn how to view and edit digital photos on your Chromebook, using the Google Photos app.

→ Viewing and Editing Photos in Chrome OS
→ Viewing and Editing Photos with Google Photos

Viewing and Editing Photos

If you take a lot of pictures with your digital camera, you want to view those photos and perhaps make a few edits. When you're using your Chromebook, you can upload and store your photos with the Google Photos app—which you also can use to perform sophisticated photo editing.

Viewing and Editing Photos in Chrome OS

Let's look first at how you can view digital photos on your Chromebook. You can view photos stored locally (in your Chromebook's long-term storage, on your camera's memory card, on a USB drive, or on an external hard drive) or online, in the cloud, with the Google Photos service.

View Photos Locally

You access photos stored on your Chromebook or on any connected storage device via the Files app.

1. Open the Files app and, in the navigation pane, click the device or folder where the photos are stored.

2. Click the thumbnail view button to view thumbnails of the stored pictures.

3. Click to select the photo you want to view.

4. Click the Open button. The photo is now displayed full screen in its own window.

5. Mouse over the photo to see the navigation controls.

6. View the next picture in this folder by clicking the right arrow or press the right-arrow button on your keyboard.

7. View the previous picture in this folder by clicking the left arrow or press the left-arrow button on your keyboard.

8. Go directly to another picture in this folder by clicking that picture's thumbnail.

9. View all the pictures in this folder in a slideshow by clicking the Slideshow button.

10. Print this photo by clicking the Print button.

11. Delete this photo by clicking the Delete button.

12. Close the photo-viewing screen by clicking the X at the top-right corner.

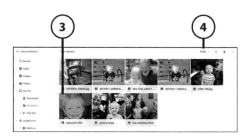

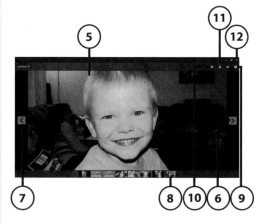

Edit Stored Photos with the Image Editor

Chrome OS includes an Image Editor with rudimentary photo-editing functionality for photos stored on your Chromebook. You can apply an "auto fix" to any photo, as well as crop, rotate, and adjust the brightness of a photo.

1. Open the picture you want to edit, mouse over the photo, and click the Edit button to display the editing controls.

2. Click Auto-Fix to apply the auto-fix control.

3. Click the Left button to rotate the picture counterclockwise.

4. Click the Right button to rotate the picture clockwise.

5. Click the Crop button to display the crop area onscreen.

6. Fix the aspect ratio for a standard photo print by clicking one of the available options—1×1, 6×4, 7×5, or 16×9.

7. Click and drag the selection to move the crop area to a different part of the photo.

8. Resize the crop area manually by clicking and dragging one of the corner selection handles.

9. Click Done to apply the crop.

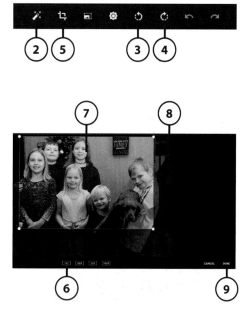

10. Adjust the brightness of the photo by clicking the Brightness button to display the Brightness and Contrast controls.

11. Increase the picture's brightness by dragging the Brightness slider to the right. To make the picture darker, drag the Brightness slider to the left.

12. Increase the contrast of the picture by dragging the Contrast slider to the right. To decrease the contrast, drag the Contrast slider to the left.

13. Click Done to apply your changes.

Viewing and Editing Photos with Google Photos

For more sophisticated photo-editing options than provided by the Chrome OS Image Editor, check out Google Photos. This is a web-based photo storage service and photo-editing app that's integrated into the Google ecosystem.

If you have an Android phone, Google Photos may be preinstalled. If so, every photo you take on your phone is automatically uploaded to Google Photos.

Even if Google Photos is not preinstalled on your phone, you can download and install it from your phone's app store. Versions are available for both Android and iPhones. You also can access Google Photos from any computer (Chromebook, Mac, or Windows) by pointing your web browser to photos.google.com.

Google Photos Storage

Google Photos offers free storage for an unlimited number of photos (and videos). Just make sure you select the High Quality option on your phone, which stores photos at a maximum 16 megapixel resolution. (This is more than good enough for most users.) If you select to upload at Original Quality, your storage space is limited.

View Photos

Google Photos is not only a full-featured photo-editing app, but it's also a great way to view all the photos you've stored online.

1. From the Google Photos main page, click Photos to view photos in reverse chronological order (newest first).

2. Click any photo to view it in the full window.

3. Mouse over the photo to display the navigational controls. Click the right arrow (or press the right-arrow key on your Chromebook keyboard) to advance to the next photo. Click the left arrow (or press the left-arrow key on the keyboard) to return to the previous photo.

4. Click the Back arrow to return to all your photos on the main screen.

5. Google Photos automatically organizes your photos into albums by content and type. Click Albums to view your photos organized into albums.

6. Click any album to view its contents.

7. Click + Create to create a new album.

8. Click Assistant to view photo creations—collages, animations, photo books, and more—created by Google Photos.

9. Click to view a specific creation.

Edit a Photo

Google Photos includes a full-featured photo editor you can use to touch up or radically edit your photos.

1. From the main Google Photos screen, click to open the photo you want to edit.

2. Click the Edit button to display the editing pane.

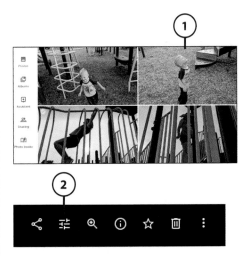

Crop and Rotate

The editing pane features three tabs. The first lets you apply various filters to your photo. The second lets you perform detailed editing. The third lets you crop and rotate your photo.

1. Open the picture for editing and then select the Crop & Rotate tab.

2. Click the Aspect Ratio button and select the desired aspect ratio, such as Square or 16:9.

3. Click and drag the crop handles until you like what you see onscreen.

4. Click the Rotate button to rotate the picture 90 degrees counter-clockwise. *Or…*

5. Click and drag the Rotate slider to rotate the picture in more discrete increments.

6. Click Done when done.

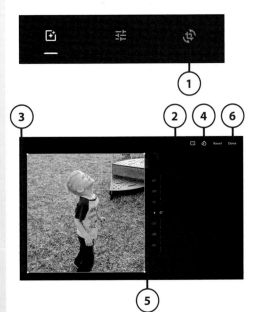

Undo Edits

If you don't like your changes to the photo, you can revert to the original by clicking Undo.

Apply a Filter

Like many camera and photo apps available for mobile phones, Google Photos lets you apply *filters* to your photos. A filter gives a photo a specific look with a single click.

1. Open the picture for editing and then select the Color Filters tab.

2. Click the Auto tile to apply an automatic "fix" of color and brightness to the photo. *Or...*

3. Click any filter to apply that filter.

4. Click Done when done.

Adjust Light Controls

When a picture is underexposed, it appears too dark. When a picture is overexposed, it appears too light. You can adjust the exposure, brightness, and contrast of any picture from within Google Photos.

1. Open the picture for editing and then select the Basic Adjustments tab.

2. Drag the Light slider to the right to brighten the picture. Drag the slider to the left to darken the picture.

3. Click the down arrow next to the Light slider to make more precise adjustments.

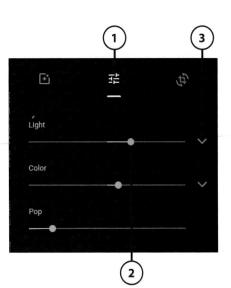

4. Drag the Exposure slider to the right to increase the picture's exposure settings (brightens the picture) or to the left to decrease the exposure settings (darkens the picture).

5. Drag the Contrast slider to increase or decrease the picture's contrast.

6. Drag the Highlights slider to adjust the brightest areas of your photo.

7. Drag the Shadows slider to adjust the darkest areas of your photo.

8. Drag the Whites slider to adjust the picture's white levels.

9. Drag the Blacks slider to adjust the picture's black levels.

10. Drag the Vignette control to the right to add a dark edge around the center of the picture.

11. Click Done when done.

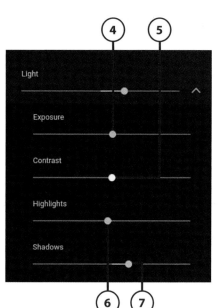

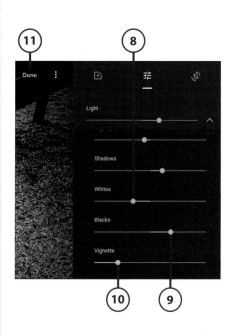

Adjust Color Controls

You can use Google Photos to adjust the saturation, tint, and other color options in a picture.

1. Open the picture for editing and then select the Basic Adjustments tab.

2. Drag the Color slider to the right to increase the overall color levels. Drag the Color slider to the left to decrease the color levels.

3. Click the down arrow next to the Color slider to make more precise adjustments.

4. Drag the Saturation slider to the right to increase the amount of color in the picture or to the left to decrease the color saturation.

5. Drag the Warmth slider to the right to make the colors warmer (reddish) or to the left to make the colors cooler (blueish).

6. Drag the Tint slider to adjust the tint of the picture.

7. Drag the Skin Tone slider to adjust the skin tones in the picture.

8. Drag the Deep Blue slider to increase or decrease the deep blue colors in the picture.

9. Click the Done button when done.

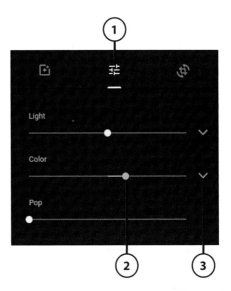

Pop

There's one more control on the Basic Adjustments tab. Drag the Pop slider to the right to make the contrast and colors of your picture "pop." (You have to try it to see how it works.)

Share a Photo

It's easy to share any photo stored in Google Photos. On your Chromebook, you can share pictures via email, Facebook, or Twitter.

1. Open the picture you want to share and then click the Share button.

2. Share via Facebook by clicking Facebook and following the onscreen instructions.

3. Share via Twitter by clicking Twitter and following the onscreen instructions.

4. Share via email by searching or browsing for the preferred contact and then selecting that person's name.

5. The selected contact is added to the panel. Click Add a Message to add a message to accompany this photo.

6. Click the Send button.

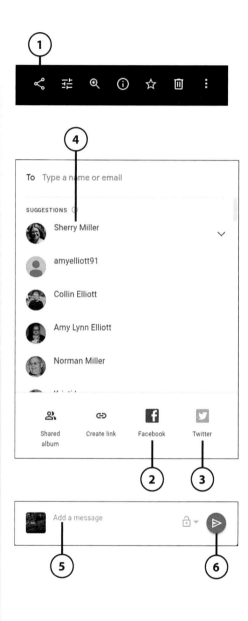

Delete a Photo

You may find that you've taken a photo
that isn't worth keeping. When you
delete a photo in Google Photos, it
is deleted from all devices using the
Google Photos app.

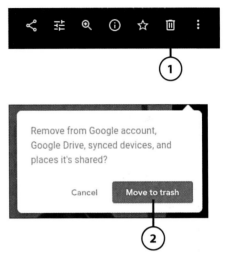

1. Open the photo you want to
    delete and then click the Delete
    (trash can) icon.

2. When prompted, click Move to
    Trash or Got It.

In this chapter, you learn how to use Google's productivity apps.

→ Getting to Know the Google Docs Suite
→ Using Docs, Sheets, and Slides

Getting Productive with Google Docs, Sheets, and Slides

When you want to get productive with your Chromebook, Google has you covered. The Google Docs suite of apps includes the Google Docs word processor, Google Sheets spreadsheet, and Google Slides presentation program. They're all free, and they all work great with any Chromebook.

Getting to Know the Google Docs Suite

The Google Docs suite includes three separate apps, all connected by a single dashboard:

- Google Docs, a word processor similar to Microsoft Word

- Google Sheets, a spreadsheet program similar to Microsoft Excel

- Google Slides, a presentation program similar to Microsoft PowerPoint

The three apps are web-based, as are all the documents they create. This means you can use the Google Docs apps on your Chromebook wherever you have an Internet connection—and on any other connected computer, smartphone, or tablet. You can also share your Google Docs documents with other users, which is great for group collaboration.

Speaking of collaboration, if you share files with people who use Microsoft Office apps, know that all of the Google Docs apps are file-compatible with Office. The Google Docs word processor can read and write Microsoft Word files, Sheets can read and write Microsoft Excel files, and Slides can read and write Microsoft PowerPoint files.

Navigate the Dashboard

You access Google Docs by launching the Google Docs app from your Chromebook. The Docs dashboard displays all the documents you've previously created with Google Docs. To open a document for editing, all you have to do is click it. The document appears in the same browser tab in the editing environment.

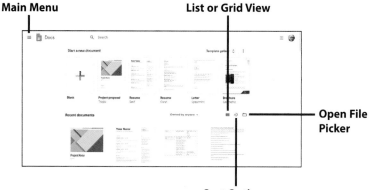

Main Menu

List or Grid View

Open File Picker

Sort Options

To switch to Docs, Sheets, or Slides view, or to adjust general settings, click the Main Menu button at the top left. To switch between list and grid views, click the List View/Grid View button. To sort files by title, last modified, last one you opened, or last one you modified, click the Sort Options button. And to open other files, click the Open File Picker button.

Open an Existing File

You access all your existing files from the Docs dashboard.

1. Click to select Docs, Sheets, or Slides files.

2. Click the file you want to open.

Create a New Document

You create new documents from the Google Docs dashboard.

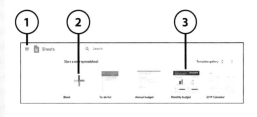

1. From the dashboard, click the main menu button to select the type of file you want to create.

2. Click the Blank (+) tile. *Or…*

3. Click a specific template to create a file like that one.

4. A new blank document opens in the same browser tab. To name this document, click Untitled Document (or Spreadsheet or Presentation) at the top of the page, just above the menu bar.

5. Enter the title for your new document and then press Enter.

Saving Your Files

It's easy to save a file in Google Docs—in fact, you don't have to do anything. That's because Docs automatically saves all files you're working on to your Google Drive online. Any time you make a change to the document, the document is automatically saved again. You don't have to do anything manually.

Import a Microsoft Office File

If you work with colleagues who use Microsoft Office, you can use Google Docs to view and edit the documents created in Word, Excel, and PowerPoint.

1. From the dashboard, click the File Picker button to open the Open a File dialog box.

2. If the document is stored on Google Drive, click My Drive and select the file.

3. If the document is stored on your Chromebook or on an external storage device, click Upload.

4. Click Select a File from Your Device to open the Files app.

5. When the Files app opens, navigate to and click the file you want to import.

6. Click the Open button. The document opens for editing in Google Docs.

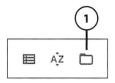

Export a File to Microsoft Office

Any Google Docs document you create can be downloaded in the appropriate Microsoft Office file format for viewing and editing by anyone using Microsoft Office.

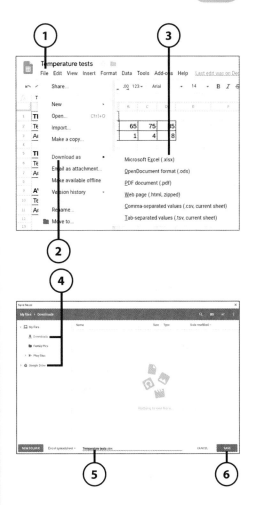

1. From within the document you want to export, click the File menu.

2. Click Download As.

3. Click Microsoft Word (.docx), Microsoft Excel (.xlsx), or Microsoft PowerPoint (.pptx).

4. When the Files app opens, select Google Drive to save to your Google Drive, Downloads to save on your Chromebook, or any attached external storage device to save there.

5. Accept or edit the suggested file name in the File Name field.

6. Click the Save button.

Print a File

Printing within Google Docs is handled by Google's Cloud Print service—which means you have to have Cloud Print configured before you start to print. (Learn more in Chapter 12, "Printing with Google Cloud Print.")

1. From within the document you want to print, click the Print button on the toolbar to open a Google Cloud Print panel.

2. If the Destination setting is not the printer you want, select another from the printer list.

3. By default, the entire document will print, but if you want to print only part of a document, go to the Pages section and enter a specific page or range of pages into the text box.

4. Click the Print button.

Print

Total: **1 sheet of paper**

Cancel Print ④

Destination 🖶 ENVY 4500 e-All-in-C ▼ ②

Pages All ③

Copies 1

Color Color ▼

More settings ⌄

Share a File with Others

Sharing a Google Docs file is similar to sharing any file on Google Drive. You have the option of letting others only view the shared document or edit it—the latter of which is what you want if you're collaborating on a group project.

1. From within the document you want to share, click the Share button to display the Share with Others pane.

2. Enter the names or email addresses of the people you want to share this document with into the People box. Separate multiple names or email addresses with commas.

3. Click the button to the right of the People box and select whether these people Can Edit, Can Comment, or Can View this document.

4. Click the Done button, and the document is shared with those selected people.

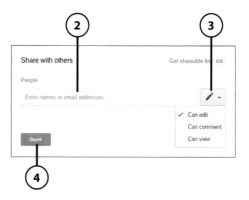

USING GOOGLE DOCS OFFLINE

Although Google Docs is a web-based app suite—which means you need to be connected to the Internet to run it—it does have a special offline mode you can use when you don't have an Internet connection handy. In this offline mode, you download your documents so you can work without a connection, and then you synchronize ("sync") your work to Google Drive the next time you're connected.

To enable offline access for Docs, Sheets, and Slides, go to the dashboard, click the Main Menu button, and then select Settings. When the Settings dialog box appears, click "on" the Offline switch and then click OK. All of your Docs, Sheets, and Slides files sync so that they're available when you don't have an Internet connection.

To use Google Docs offline, just launch the Docs, Sheets, or Slides app, open a file, and start working. The next time you connect to the Internet, the changes you've made automatically synchronize with the versions of those files stored online in Google Drive. You don't have to do anything, manually, to make this happen—it all occurs in the background.

Using Docs, Sheets, and Slides

The three main Google Docs apps behave very much like any other word processor, spreadsheet, or presentation program. There are drop-down menus at the top of each window and a toolbar of common tasks beneath that. You edit directly into the currently open document and then perform app-specific tasks as you will.

Word Processing with Google Docs

The Google Docs word processor app (yes, it shares the same name as the larger Google Docs suite) looks a lot like Microsoft Word—or at least an older version of Word, before it went to the "ribbon" interface. You have a big blank space to create your document, a drop-down menu bar, and a toolbar with common commands. It's pretty familiar-looking and fairly easy to use.

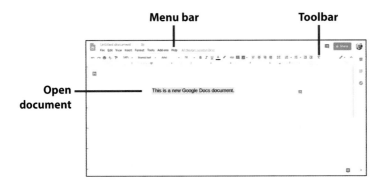

Table 18.1 details how to perform common tasks.

Table 18.1   Common Google Docs Tasks

Task	Do this
Enter text	Use your mouse or keyboard arrow keys to position the cursor and then start typing.
Copy text	Use the cursor to select the text; then click Edit, Copy or press Ctrl+C.
Cut text	Use the cursor to select the text; then click Edit, Cut or press Ctrl+X.
Paste text	Move the cursor to where you want to insert the cut or copied text; then click Edit, Paste or press Ctrl+V.
Format text	Use the cursor to select the text; then click the appropriate formatting button on the toolbar.
Format paragraph	Position the cursor anywhere in the paragraph; then click the appropriate formatting button on the toolbar.
Apply text styles	Position the cursor anywhere in the paragraph; then click the Styles button on the toolbar and make a selection.

Number Crunching with Google Sheets

Just as the Google Docs app resembles a web-based version of the Microsoft Word word processor, Google Sheets is a web-based spreadsheet app that works much like Microsoft Excel. You use Sheets to work with numbers—including writing complex formulas and using predefined functions.

Formula bar   **Menu bar**   **Toolbar**

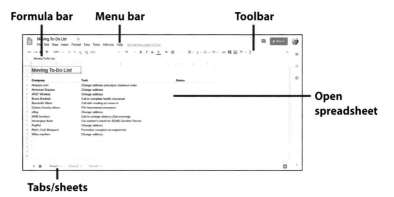

Open spreadsheet

Tabs/sheets

Table 18.2 details how to perform common tasks.

Table 18.2   Common Google Sheets Tasks

Task	Do this
Enter data	Move to the cell where you want to enter data and start typing. Press Enter when done.
Edit data	Select the cell to edit. Click within the Formula bar and edit contents. Press Enter when done.
Select a row	Click the row header on the left.
Select a column	Click the column header above.
Create a new tab/sheet	Click the + button at the bottom of the current sheet.
Rename a sheet	Double-click the sheet, type a new name, and then press Enter.
Format cell data	Select the cell(s); then click the appropriate formatting button on the toolbar.
Format numbers	Select the cell(s); then click the desired number format on the toolbar.
Format cell color	Select the cell(s), click the Fill Color button, and then click the color you want.
Format cell borders	Select the cell(s), click the Borders button, and then click the desired border style.
Enter a formula	Select the cell, type =, and then type the formula. You can enter specific numbers, one or more cell references, or mathematical operators. For example, to add the contents of cells A1 and A2, enter the formula =A1+A2.
Use a function	Select the cell, click the Functions button, and then select a common function. (To apply a different function, click Functions and then select More Functions.) Enter the necessary cell references for this function; then press Enter.
Create a chart	Select the cells that contain the data you want to chart. Click the Insert Chart button on the toolbar to display the Chart Editor pane. Select one of the recommended charts; then click the Insert button.

Presenting with Google Slides

Google Slides is Google's presentation app, similar in functionality to Microsoft PowerPoint. You use Google Slides to create and give onscreen presentations.

Menu bar   Toolbar

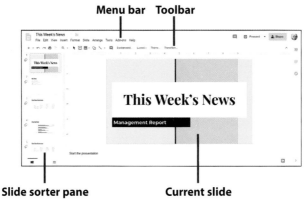

Slide sorter pane   **Current slide**

Table 18.3 details how to perform common tasks.

Table 18.3   Common Google Slides Tasks

Task	Do this
Add a new slide	In the slide sorter pane, click the slide after which you want the new slide to appear. Click the down arrow next to the New Slide (+) button on the toolbar; then select the slide layout you want.
Delete a slide	In the slide sorter pane, click the slide you want to delete; then click the File menu and select Move to Trash.
Rearrange slides	In the slide sorter pane, click and drag a slide up or down to a new position.
Add text	In the current slide, click to select any text object and then start typing.
Format text	In the current slide, select the text to format and then click the appropriate formatting controls in the toolbar.
Add an image	Position the cursor where you want to insert the image; then click the Image button to open the Insert Image panel. Select the Upload tab and click Choose an Image to Upload. When the Files app opens, select an image and click Open. To resize the image, click and drag the corner handles.
Choose a new theme	Click the Theme button to open the Choose a Theme panel, click the theme you want, and then click OK.

Task	Do this
Add custom background color or graphic	Click the Background button to open the Background dialog box. Click the Color to control to choose a background color. To use a background image, click the Choose button in the image button and select an image.
Add transitions between slides	In the slide sorter pane, click the desired slide. Click the Transition button to display the Animations pane; then click the Transition Type button and select the desired transition.
Present your presentation	Click the down arrow next to the Present button and select Present from Beginning. Click the next-slide (right) arrow or press the right-arrow key on your keyboard to advance to the next slide.

>>>Go Further

USING MICROSOFT OFFICE ONLINE

The Google Docs suite isn't the only web-based productivity tool you can use on your Chromebook. Microsoft has online versions of its entire Office suite, including Word (word processing), Excel (spreadsheet), and PowerPoint (presentations).

Obviously, a web-based version of Office has appeal to the hundreds of millions of people who use the traditional Office software. If you work with or for an organization that has standardized on Microsoft Office, this option is preferred to using the Google Docs suite.

Also appealing is the price. Microsoft Office Online is completely free, unlike the more expensive software versions.

Note, however, that the individual apps in Office Online don't come with all the power features of the software versions. In this aspect, Office Online resembles Google Docs; average users will find all the features they need, whereas power users might need more sophisticated functionality.

You can access Office Online from within the Chrome browser, at www.office.com. You can also download Office Online apps from the Google Play Store.

Booktrack · Classroom · Duolingo

Grammaropo... · Grasshopper · Kids A-Z

19

Using Chromebooks in Education

Chromebooks are popular among all types of users, but especially so with schools and educators. An increasingly large number of elementary schools, middle schools, and high schools are distributing Chromebooks to their students to help them complete and enhance their schoolwork. If you have a child in school today, chances are he or she is using a Chromebook in the classroom!

Why Schools Like Chromebooks

Schools at all levels have been adopting technology to help educate their students for several decades now. From the dawn of the personal computer era to today, teachers and students have used computers and tablets to make learning more fun and effective.

When it comes to technology in the classroom, Apple has long been one of the most successful companies. When Apple released its first iPad tablet, it got a tremendous response from school districts across the country and around the world; teachers recognized how easy it was to use an iPad, and how they could use it to teach technology to their students. For many educators, it was a notably better option than using the more complicated Windows-based personal computers of the day.

It didn't take long, however, for schools to recognize the iPad's limitations. First, the lack of a keyboard made it more difficult to do input-heavy tasks. Second, Apple's closed infrastructure made it difficult to manage large numbers of iPads in a typical school installation. And third, there was the cost—at $400 or more a pop, equipping every student with an iPad was a pricey proposition.

This explains why, over the past several years, more and more school districts have been trading in their iPads for Google Chromebooks. More than 30 million students today use a Chromebook at school, making the Chromebook the dominant computing device in education. Google now owns 60% of the K–12 school market, easily surpassing Microsoft's 22% and Apple's 18% shares.

Why do schools like Chromebooks? It's for all the reasons they no longer fancy iPads. Chromebooks are true productivity devices, thanks to the built-in keyboard and bigger screen. They're easier to manage across a school or school district because the entire OS is web-based. They're a lot, lot lower priced than Apple's tablets. And any student can use any Chromebook; as a "zero state" device, any student can log on to any Chromebook with their personal account and see their desktop and apps. (iPads, on the other hand, are inextricably linked to a single user account.)

And it's not just the bureaucrats and IT folks who like Chromebooks. Students overwhelmingly prefer the laptop form factor over that of keyboardless tablets. It's a lot easier to search Google, write papers, and even enter programming code on a real keyboard than on a touchscreen.

For these reasons and more, Google is winning the hearts and minds of teachers and students across the country. It's likely that at least some of the children in your neighborhood are familiar with Chromebooks—and like them!

Using Google's Tools for Education

In addition to the multitude of educational apps available for Chromebooks, Google also offers a set of educational tools that teachers and students can use to manage their assignments, tests, projects, and such. The two primary tools are G Suite for Education and Google Classroom.

G Suite for Education

G Suite for Education is a suite of collaborative tools designed for both educators and students. Schools or school districts sign up for their teachers and students to use the suite of apps.

The table describes the apps in G Suite for Education. Learn more about G Suite for Education at edu.google.com/products/gsuite-for-education/.

Gmail	Email
Google Calendar	Web-based calendar
Google Classroom	Tool for teachers to use to create assignments and communicate with students
Google Docs, Sheets, and Slides	Word processing, spreadsheet, and presentation apps
Google Drive	Cloud-based storage
Google Forms	Tool for creating forms, quizzes, and surveys
Google Groups	Topic-focused online message boards
Google Hangouts Meet	Secure video calls and messaging
Google Jamboard	Cloud-based interactive whiteboard
Google Sites	Tool that teachers can use to build websites for their classes
Google Vault	Tool for managing settings for students and their devices

Google Classroom

Google Classroom is a free tool that teachers can use to streamline the process of sharing files between teachers and students. By doing this, Google Classroom simplifies creating, distributing, and grading assignments in a totally paperless fashion.

Google Classroom —

Teachers use Google Classroom to distribute assignments, manage student responses, and communicate with their students. Students use Google Classroom to retrieve, complete, and upload completed assignments, as well as communicate with teachers and other students. It's an essential tool for communication and classroom management.

Learn more at classroom.google.com.

Popular Educational Apps

When it comes to learning on Chromebooks, the sky's the limit. There's an app for just about every topic in a school's curriculum, designed for students at all grade levels.

With that in mind, here's a quick look at some of the more popular educational Chromebook apps you'll find in use in schools across the nation.

Booktrack Classroom

Booktrack Classroom

This app is essentially an enhanced e-book reader. Grade-appropriate books are accompanied by suitable audio soundtracks—music, sound effects, and more. Learn more at www.booktrackclassroom.com.

Duolingo

Duolingo —
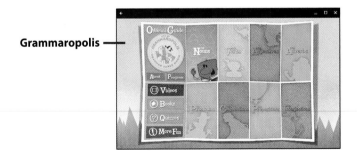

Students use Duolingo to learn new languages. Lessons incorporate fun games to make learning more approachable. Students set daily goals and earn colorful badges and rewards. Languages include French, German, Italian, and (for non-English speakers) English.

Learn more at www.duolingo.com.

Grammaropolis

Grammaropolis —

Grammaropolis offers a variety of e-books, videos, quizzes, games, and apps to help students learn and perfect their grammar skills. Learn more at www.grammaropolis.com.

Grasshopper

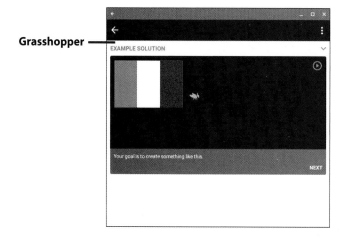

Grasshopper teaches kids how to code in a visual programming environment. Students solve visual puzzles to learn basic coding concepts, then develop their own apps and games using JavaScript.

Learn more at https://grasshopper.codes/.

Raz-Kids

Raz-Kids is a first-class online guided reading program and part of the Kids A–Z app. Students read e-books at their own pace at their individual reading level. Learn more at www.raz-kids.com.

>>>*Go Further*

MORE ON THE WEB

Many schools use educational websites that don't necessarily have Chrome apps. Instead, they have their students use the Chrome browser on their Chromebooks to access these sites.

For example, CK-12 (www.ck12.org) is a popular education site that offers textbooks and online learning materials on a variety of math, science, and English topics, with a strong focus on STEM education. And Dreambox Learning (www.dreambox.com) is an online K–8 math site that offers adaptive quizzes and lessons for self-paced learning.

There are also websites for managing classwork and assignments, such as Infinite Campus (www.infinitecampus.com) and Schoology (www.schoology.com). Check with your local school system to see which apps and sites they use for their students and teachers.

Task Manager - Google Chrome

Task ▲	Memory footprint	CPU	Network	Process ID
App: com.android.settings	–	0.0	0	22787
App: com.android.vending	–	0.0	0	23871
App: com.area120.grasshopper	–	13.0	0	2786
App: com.duolingo	–	0.0	0	4529
App: com.google.android.apps.classroom	–	0.0	0	2506
App: com.google.android.gms.ui	–	0.0	0	988

End process

In this chapter, you learn how to make your Chromebook run more efficiently, as well as how to deal with potential problems.

→ Using Chrome Safely and Securely
→ Optimizing Your Chromebook's Performance
→ Troubleshooting Chromebook Problems

20

Optimizing and Troubleshooting Your Chromebook

How do you keep your Chromebook operating in tip-top condition? It's a matter of working safely and smartly, optimizing a handful of settings, and knowing what to do when things go wrong.

Using Chrome Safely and Securely

Many users are embracing Chromebooks because of security issues. That is, using a Chromebook with web-based storage is safer and more secure than using a traditional PC with local storage. You don't have to worry about computer viruses, spyware, and such; you don't even have to worry about someone hacking into your computer and stealing your data. This security inherent in the Chrome model is great, but there are things you can do to make your Chromebook even safer and more secure. It's a matter of practicing safe computing—and knowing all your options.

Chrome OS and Malware

Why are Chromebooks more secure than Windows or Mac computers? It's simple; because your Chromebook can't download, store, or run traditional applications, that also means it can't download malware—at all.

With a Chromebook, unlike any other form of personal computer, there's absolutely zero chance you'll run into computer viruses, spyware, and the like. Apple may talk about having less malware than Windows, but you can still hack into the Mac OS. You simply can't hack into Chrome OS; there's nothing on your Chromebook to infect.

So, with a Chromebook, you *don't* have to install antivirus, anti-spyware, or firewall programs. These tools aren't necessary because a Chromebook simply can't download and run malware programs. In fact, your Chromebook can't download executable programs of any type, so you're extremely safe from this sort of attack. There are no viruses, spyware, or other infiltrations possible with the Chrome OS.

Chromebooks Are Safe

Bottom line: There's no safer computer out there than a Chromebook.

Protect Against Phishing

Although Chrome OS and your Chromebook are, by design, virtually invulnerable to malware-based attacks, there's still the issue of those intrusions that depend on the human element to succeed. That is, when it comes to online scams, your Chromebook can't protect you from yourself.

One of the most common forms of online scams involves something called *phishing*, where a fraudster tries to extract valuable information from you via a series of fake email messages and websites.

Most phishing scams start with an email message. A phishing email is designed to look like an official email, but is in reality a clever forgery, down to the use of the original firm's logo. The goal of the email is to get you to click an enclosed link that purports to take you to an "official" website. That website, however, is also fake. Any information you provide to that website is used for various types of fraud, from simple username/password theft to credit card and identity theft.

Of course, there's little Google can do to protect you from yourself; the best defense against phishing scams is simple common sense. That is, you should never click through a link in an email message that asks for any type of personal information—whether that be your bank account number or eBay password or whatever. Even if the email *looks* official, it probably isn't; legitimate institutions and websites never include this kind of link in their official messages. If you don't click to the phishing site, you're safe.

Fortunately, Google Chrome includes anti-phishing technology that can detect most phishing websites. If you navigate to a known phishing website, Chrome displays a warning message instead of the suspect web page. When you see this warning message in the Chrome browser, navigate away from the troublesome web page as quickly as possible.

Don't Save Passwords

By default, Chrome offers to save the passwords you use to log on to various websites. However, if another user logs on to your Chromebook using your Google Account, they'll be able to access these password-protected sites without your knowledge or permission. It's safer, then, to *not* have Chrome save passwords.

1. Click anywhere in the System Tray to display the Quick Settings panel.

2. Click Settings to display the Settings page.

3. Go to the Autofill section and click Passwords.

4. Switch "off" Offer to Save Passwords.

5. Switch "off" Auto Sign-In.

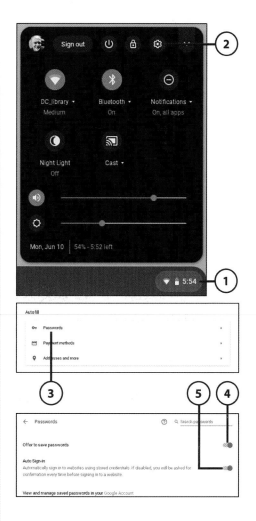

Don't Use Autofill

Similarly, Chrome's Autofill feature automatically saves the personal data you enter into web forms to be used for later automatic entry. If you want to be sure that other unauthorized users don't have access to this web form data, you want to turn off the Autofill feature.

1. On the Settings page, go to the Autofill section and click Addresses and More.

2. Click "off" Save and Fill Addresses.

Restrict Sign-In

There's one last setting you should consider. By default, anyone with a Google Account can log in to your Chromebook, and then log in to their own personal data and settings. You may not want just anyone to use your Chromebook, however; to that end, you can limit use to only those people you preselect.

1. On the Settings page, go to the People section and click Manage Other People.

2. Switch "on" the Restrict Sign-In to the Following Users switch.

3. Click Add Person to add a user to the restricted sign-in list.

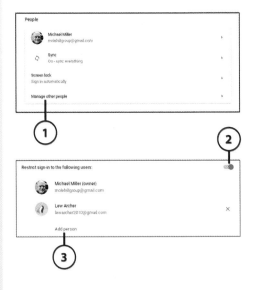

Optimizing Your Chromebook's Performance

Out of the box, a Chromebook is a very fast computer with a very long battery life. There are things you can do, however, to make it run ever faster—and last longer on a charge.

Optimize Battery Life

Let's start with your Chromebook's battery life. On average, you're going to get 8–10 hours per charge, depending on the model, which is pretty good. Your battery may last longer, however, if you take the appropriate precautions:

- **Use the right adapter.** Use only the charger/adapter supplied by your Chromebook's manufacturer, or an authorized replacement. Using the wrong charger/adapter can negatively impact the life of your battery—or even damage the Chromebook itself.

- **Keep it cool.** Batteries don't like heat. The hotter the room, the less the battery will hold its charge—and the increased likelihood you'll damage the Chromebook. Worst-case scenario, your Chromebook will get hot enough to catch fire. This is not desirable. It's best to keep your Chromebook as near room temperature as possible, even when it's not in use.

- **Keep a little charge.** When you're not using your Chromebook for an extended period, charge the battery to about the 30%–40% level. This level of charge will maintain battery performance as best as possible.

- **Dim the screen.** When running your Chromebook on battery power, turn down the screen brightness. A brighter screen draws more power, and runs the battery down faster.

- **Disable Wi-Fi.** If you're not working online, turn off Wi-Fi functionality. Your Chromebook's wireless receiver draws a lot of power. (Of course, your Chromebook is fairly useless if it's not connected to the Internet, so this may not be a viable option.)

>>>Go Further

BATTERY REPLACEMENT

All batteries get weaker over time. If your battery life starts to deteriorate, or if your battery stops working altogether, you need to replace it with a new battery.

Unfortunately, the battery is sealed into your Chromebook; it's not user replaceable. To remove or replace your Chromebook's internal battery, you need to take it or send it to an authorized service center.

That said, you can find lots of videos on YouTube that explain how to replace the battery. You probably shouldn't do it, however—at least with newer Chromebooks. Changing the battery on your own voids any remaining warranty for your device.

Speed Up Performance

On a traditional computer, you can speed up performance by managing how programs use the PC's memory and hard disk. Because most Chromebooks don't have hard disks, there isn't much to manage there—which is one of the reasons a Chromebook is so fast by default.

There are a few things you can do, however, to speed up the performance of your Chromebook. Because most of what you do will be web-based, most of these tricks involve how you browse online:

- **Don't multitask.** Each web app that's running takes up processor capacity, memory, and upload/download bandwidth. If multiple apps are running simultaneously, in multiple browser tabs or windows, that can really slow down your Chromebook's processing—and clog up your Internet connection. This can even be the case if some of those apps are running in the background, like a real-time weather or stock app. Bottom line, if you don't want your Chromebook to become too sluggish, close some of those browser tabs.

- **Disable DNS prefetching.** When configured properly, the Chrome browser can "prefetch" all the URLs on each web page you load, essentially looking them up in advance in the event you click them. This speeds up the loading of any subsequent pages you click to, which results in faster browsing. To enable DNS prefetching, open the Settings page, click Advanced, go to the Privacy and Security section, and click "off" the Use a Prediction Service to Load Pages More Quickly option.

Troubleshooting Chromebook Problems

Your Chromebook is much more reliable than a traditional personal computer. The lack of any moving parts (no hard drive or optical drive) enhances reliability, and the technical compactness of Chrome OS (no legacy stuff to support) means there's less stuff to go wrong.

That doesn't mean you'll never encounter any problems, however; there are still times when a particular app or web page or even your entire Chromebook might freeze. Fortunately, your Chromebook's inherent simplicity makes it easy to troubleshoot and recover from even the most significant issues.

Deal with a Frozen App or Web Page

Perhaps the most common problem you're likely to encounter is a frozen application or web page—that is, the tab you're currently on doesn't respond to anything you do. Sometimes you can navigate off this tab to another tab or window, sometimes not; but in any case, you're left with one nonresponsive tab.

When this happens, you can undertake the following steps to close the tab and resume your other work:

1. Start by simply trying to close the tab. Click the X on the tab itself, or select the tab and then press Ctrl+W (or do both).

2. If the tab is still frozen, you can try shutting down the window it's in by pressing Ctrl+Shift+W. (This only works if you have more than one window open.)

3. If that doesn't work, press Search+Esc (or click the Customize and Control button and select More Tools, Task Manager) to open the Chrome Task Manager. All running tasks (apps, pages, extensions, and so forth) are listed in the Task Manager window. To close the frozen task, click that task and then click the End Process button.

Task Manager
Chrome OS features a Task Manager, similar to the one in Microsoft Windows. You use the Task Manager to review all running tasks and services—and to shut down tasks that won't close of their own accord.

---

4. If the tab still won't close, you need to shut down and then restart your Chromebook. Press and hold the Power button for about 8 seconds until your Chromebook completely powers off—then restart your Chromebook and get back to work.

Reset Your Chromebook

Although most of the data you use on your Chromebook is stored in the cloud, some personal data (primarily about user accounts) is stored locally. Sometimes this locally stored data can become corrupted, causing your Chromebook to misbehave.

When this happens, you can often get things working again by resetting your Chromebook to its original condition—what Google calls *powerwashing*. This is different from the Restore option, which restores all settings to their defaults while keeping all user data; powerwashing also restores default settings but also clears all your local data from the Chromebook, leaving you with a factory-fresh machine.

1. From the Settings window, click Advanced, scroll to the Reset Settings section, and then click Powerwash.

2. When the Restart Your Device dialog box appears, click the Restart button.

This restarts your Chromebook, with all local data deleted. Follow the instructions in Chapter 2, "Unboxing and Setting Up Your New Chromebook," to create a new user account and set up your Chromebook from scratch.

Reset from the Sign-In Screen

You can also reset your Chromebook from the sign-in screen. Just press Ctrl+Alt+Shift+R and then click Restart.

It's Not All Good

The Downside of Resetting

When you reset your Chromebook, you not only clear usernames and logon information, you also delete any other data saved on your Chromebook. This includes photos, downloaded files, saved networks, and the like. All data for all accounts is deleted. The next time you start up your Chromebook will be just like the first time; you'll be prompted to create a new user account, and so forth.

>>>Go Further

UPDATING CHROME OS

One of the nice things about using a cloud-based operating system like Chrome OS is that it's constantly updated without much effort on your part. When a new update is available, your Chromebook will be updated the next time you connect to the Internet.

Know, however, that updates are provided only for a set number of years. Every Chromebook model has an Auto Update Expiration (AUE) date. In most instances, this is six and a half years after the introduction of a hardware platform. If you purchase a Chromebook near the start of its model life, you'll get most of that six and a half years; if you purchase an older Chromebook released later in its model life, you won't get as much life out of it.

When a Chromebook passes its AUE date, it still continues to work; it just doesn't receive any more automatic updates. Learn more and view your device's AUE date at https://support.google.com/chrome/a/answer/6220366.

A

Google Chrome Keyboard Shortcuts

A *keyboard shortcut* is a combination of two or more keyboard buttons that you use to perform specific actions within Google Chrome. Using keyboard shortcuts can be a real time saver.

Navigation and Browser Shortcuts

Keyboard Shortcut	Action
Ctrl+Alt+/	Display list of keyboard shortcuts
Ctrl+O	Open a file
Alt+Shift+M	Open the Files app
Search+Esc	Open Task Manager
Ctrl+H	Open History page
Ctrl+J	Open Downloads page
Alt+E	Open Customize and Control menu
Ctrl+Shift+B	Toggle Bookmarks bar on or off
Ctrl+Full Screen	Configure external monitor
Ctrl+Alt+Z	Enable/disable accessibility settings (if you're not logged in to a Google Account)
Ctrl+Shift+Q	Sign out of your Google Account
Ctrl+?	Go to Help Center

Tab and Window Navigation Shortcuts

Keyboard Shortcut	Action
Ctrl+T	Open a new tab
Ctrl+W	Close the current tab
Ctrl+Shift+T	Reopen the last tab you closed
Ctrl+Tab	Go to next tab
Ctrl+Shift+Tab	Go to previous tab
Ctrl+1 through Ctrl+8	Go to the specified tab
Ctrl+9	Go to the last tab
Ctrl+N	Open a new window
Ctrl+Shift+N	Open a new window in Incognito mode
Ctrl+Shift+W	Close the current window
Alt+Tab	Go to next window
Alt+Shift+Tab	Go to previous window
Alt+1 through Alt+8	Go to the specified window
Alt+9	Go to the last open window

Keyboard Shortcut	Action
Alt+–	Minimize window
Alt+=	Maximize window
Alt+Shift and +	Center current window
Click and hold Back or Forward button in browser toolbar	See browsing history for that tab
Backspace or Alt+Left Arrow	Go to previous page in browsing history
Shift+Backspace or Alt+Right Arrow	Go to next page in browsing history
Ctrl+click a link	Open link in new tab in background
Ctrl+Shift+click a link	Open link in new tab in foreground
Shift+click a link	Open link in new window
Drag a link to a tab	Open link in the tab
Drag a link to a blank area on the tab strip	Open link in new tab
Type URL in Address bar and then press Alt+Enter	Open URL in new tab
Press Esc while dragging a tab	Return tab to its original position

Page Shortcuts

Keyboard Shortcut	Action
Alt+Up Arrow	Page up
Alt+Down Arrow	Page down
Spacebar	Scroll down web page
Ctrl+Alt+Up Arrow	Home
Ctrl+Alt+Down Arrow	End
Ctrl+P	Print page
Ctrl+S	Save page
Ctrl+R	Reload page
Ctrl+Shift+R	Reload page without using cached content
Esc	Stop loading current page
Ctrl and +	Zoom in
Ctrl and –	Zoom out
Ctrl+0	Reset zoom level

Keyboard Shortcut	Action
Ctrl+D	Save page as bookmark
Ctrl+Shift+D	Save all open pages in window as bookmarks in a new folder
Drag a link to Bookmarks bar	Save link as bookmark
Ctrl+F	Search current page
Ctrl+G or Enter	Go to next match for page search
Ctrl+Shift+G or Shift+Enter	Go to previous match for page search
Ctrl+K or Ctrl+E	Search Web
Ctrl+Enter	Add www. and .com to input in Address bar and open resulting URL
Ctrl+Next Window	Take a screenshot of current screen
Ctrl+U	View page source
Ctrl+Shift+I	Toggle display of Developer Tools panel
Ctrl+Shift+J	Toggle display of the DOM Inspector

Text Editing Shortcuts

Keyboard Shortcut	Description
Ctrl+A	Select everything on page
Ctrl+L or Alt+D	Select content in Omnibox
Ctrl+Shift+Right Arrow	Select next word or letter
Ctrl+Shift+Left Arrow	Select previous word or letter
Ctrl+Right Arrow	Move to start of next word
Ctrl+Left Arrow	Move to start of previous word
Ctrl+C	Copy selected content to clipboard
Ctrl+V	Paste content from clipboard
Ctrl+Shift+V	Paste content from clipboard as plain text
Ctrl+X	Cut
Ctrl+Backspace	Delete previous word
Alt+Backspace	Delete next letter
Ctrl+Z	Undo last action

Chrome Settings

The Chrome OS features a number of settings you can configure to personalize your Chromebook use. You display these settings by clicking within the System Tray and selecting Settings. (You may have to click Advanced on the Settings page to see some of these settings.)

Privacy and Security Settings

Chrome OS includes a bevy of small but important settings you can configure to increase your online privacy and security. You find these settings in the Privacy and Security section of the Settings page.

Google Chrome Privacy Settings

Setting	Description	Recommendation
Use a Prediction Service to Help Complete Searches and URLs Typed in the Address Bar or the App Launcher Search Box	By default, Google suggests queries when you start typing a search into Chrome's Omnibox.	Because this feature sends a detailed history of your web searching to Google, you can increase your privacy by disabling this setting—and not letting Google track your search behavior.
Use a Web Service to Help Resolve Navigation Errors	When this feature is enabled, Google suggests alternative pages if you encounter an incorrect or nonworking URL.	When enabled, this feature sends every URL you enter to Google, where it could be stored and used for other purposes. Google doesn't need to do this, and you can figure out your own errors; for increased privacy, disable this setting.
Safe Browsing	Protects you and your Chromebook by displaying warnings when you attempt to visit potentially dangerous sites or download dangerous files. It works by comparing the URLs you enter with a database of known suspicious websites.	Although Chrome may send some subset of the URL you enter to Google, Google never sees the full URL and doesn't track your browsing history. Because of the valuable protection offered, this is a good feature to keep enabled.
Help Improve Safe Browsing	Sends system information and page content to Google.	Although this option does help Google improve its Safe Browsing feature, it uses system resources and could potentially compromise your privacy. Consider disabling this setting.
Automatically Send Diagnostic and Usage Data to Google	By default, Google receives reports about how you use Chrome and the sites you visit.	Diagnostic and usage data? That means Google receives a copy of everything you do in Chrome. You can increase your privacy by disabling this setting and not letting Google track all your actions.

Setting	Description	Recommendation
Use a Web Service to Help Resolve Spelling Errors	This setting adds spell checking to Chrome, using the same spell-checking technology employed by Google search.	When this option is enabled, anything you type into the Chrome browser is sent to Google's servers for evaluation. Not only can this slow down your browsing, it's also sending more personal data to Google. Although it appears to (and may) be useful, it's best not to enable this setting.
Send a "Do Not Track" Request with Your Browsing Traffic	This technology lets you opt out of tracking by websites you don't actually visit— advertising networks, analytic services, and the like.	When you enable this option, you get fewer entities tracking your web browsing—which is a good thing, privacy-wise.
Allow Sites to Check if You Have Payment Methods Saved	If you configure Google to save payment methods for auto entry, this setting lets sites check to see if you have these settings saved.	While this setting may make online shopping and bill payment more convenient, it poses a very real security risk. Consider disabling.
Use a Prediction Service to Load Pages More Quickly	When this feature is enabled, Google "prefetches" all the URLs on each web page you load, essentially looking them up in advance, in the event you click them. This should speed up the loading of any subsequent pages you click to.	This is a fairly harmless option, at least in terms of privacy. Because it can, in theory, speed up your browsing, it's a good option to enable.
Enable Verified Access	Verified Access enables your Chromebook to certify that certain cryptographic keys are protected by the Chrome hardware. To do this, Verified Access sends hardware information to a Google server.	When this setting is activated, Google's server can identify your Chromebook, although it can't identify you as a user. You should disable this setting unless you're using a Chromebook supplied by an employer that uses the Verified Access feature.
Leave Wi-Fi on During Sleep	This setting keeps your Chromebook connected even in sleep mode.	Disabling this setting means that your Chromebook and the apps you're using can't receive updates when the Chromebook is in sleep mode, only when you're using it. For convenience sake, enable this setting.

Website Content Settings

Chrome also includes more than a dozen settings that determine what content is displayed in the web browser. To access these settings, open the Settings page, go to the Privacy and Security section, and select Site Settings.

Google Chrome Content Settings

Setting	Description	Recommendation
Cookies	Cookies are small files that websites store on your computer to track your browsing behavior. You can opt to allow cookies (default) or block all cookies. You also can allow cookies except from third-party sites or clear cookies when you close your browser.	As onerous as cookies sound, they help make it easier to revisit your favorite sites. However, you can increase your privacy by blocking all cookies, or by clearing cookies when you close your browser (log off from Chrome). Know, however, that without cookies, you'll need to re-enter all your personal data each time you visit a website.
Location	Some websites can serve up a more personalized experience if they know where you're located.	Do you really want all the sites you visit to know where you are? You can increase your privacy by turning off location tracking, or at least forcing sites to ask you before they track.
Camera	Some sites and services, such as Google Duo, use your Chromebook's built-in webcam.	The best option here is to select Ask Before Accessing. This way you can still use your camera when you want, but it won't be activated without your knowledge.
Microphone	Some sites and services use your Chromebook's built-in microphone to listen to you or other sounds.	As with the Camera option, the best option is to select Ask Before Accessing.
Notifications	Some websites display desktop notifications of various activities.	By default, a site has to ask for permission to display notifications. You can opt to allow or not allow such notifications.
JavaScript	JavaScript is a kind of programming language used to create certain website content. Unfortunately, JavaScript can be used to run malicious scripts in your browser—although that's much less likely or dangerous in the Chrome OS than it is on other platforms.	Although you can increase security by not running JavaScript, this can make some websites less functional. Because Chrome OS is fairly protected against malicious code, this setting is probably safe to leave enabled.

Setting	Description	Recommendation
Flash	Flash is an increasingly outmoded technology used by some older sites to display videos or active content.	You don't want Flash sites to play automatically. Instead, select the Ask First option.
Images	You can opt to show all images on web pages or not to show any images.	Not showing images speeds up web browsing, but decreases the usability of many sites.
Pop-ups and Redirects	Pop-up windows are a particularly pernicious form of unwanted online advertising. Most people hate them.	You can make your web browsing less annoying by letting Chrome block all pop-ups. (This is the default setting.)
Ads	Chrome includes a basic ad blocker that won't display intrusive or misleading ads from selected sites.	Enable this one, but also consider installing a stronger third-party ad blocker.
Background Sync	When activated, enables recently closed sites to finish sending or receiving data.	With this option disabled, you may end up with unfinished processes if you exit from a page too early. It's recommended to enable this setting.
Sound	Some web pages play music and other sounds when you open them. You can opt to automatically play this audio or not.	Not playing sounds speeds up web browsing a little, but it decreases the usability of many sites. It's recommended to enable this setting—although you can configure Chrome to mute the sound on sites you manually select.
Automatic Downloads	These controls affect how files are downloaded on your Chromebook.	By default, a site must ask to download files automatically (after the first file). You can allow or disallow this type of automatic file downloading.
Unsandboxed Plugin Access	Chrome's sandbox mode protects your computer by limiting what websites can access your computer.	By default, sites can ask to use a plug-in to access your computer. You can allow or disallow all such requests.
Handlers	Handlers enable websites to perform certain actions when links on their sites are clicked.	By default, sites are allowed to ask you if you want to perform a certain action when a link is clicked. You can disable this functionality and block all such requests.
MIDI Devices	You can connect MIDI musical devices to your Chromebook via USB; this setting determines how websites can access any connected MIDI devices.	The best setting here is to make sites ask before they access any MIDI devices. It's a better option than blocking all access completely.

Setting	Description	Recommendation
Zoom Levels	Some websites may seek to control the zoom level on your Chromebook screen.	You can manage which sites are allowed/disallowed to control this function.
USB Devices	Some websites, such as cloud storage services, might try to access USB devices connected to your Chromebook.	You can disable all web-based access to connected USB devices, or require sites to ask before you grant access. The latter option is more practical and just as safe.
PDF Documents	When you open a web page that contains a PDF document, you can opt to either open the document in Chrome or download it to your Chromebook.	Either option here is fine, although viewing PDF files in the Chrome browser is probably more convenient for most users.
Protected Content	Some sites and services use machine identifiers to uniquely identify your computer in order to authorize access to protected content such as movies or music that you've purchased.	By default, these types of identifiers are allowed. You can turn off this setting, however, or allow exceptions to the general rule.
Clipboard	Believe it or not, but some websites might try to access text and images you've cut or copied to your Chromebook's clipboard.	You can block all website access to your clipboard or require sites to ask first. The latter is the most practical option, although one could argue that blocking all clipboard access is safest.
Payment Handlers	A payment handler is software used to make online payments. Some online retailers and payment services want to install payment handler software on your Chromebook to facilitate future purchases and payments.	If you disable this setting, you may not be able to make payments on some websites. That said, disabling payment handlers is a safer option, even if it takes away much of the functionality of online shopping and payments.

C

Searching with the Chrome Browser

As discussed in Chapter 7, "Using the Chrome Browser," Google Chrome's Omnibox functions not only as an Address box but also as a search box for searching the Web. That is, you also can use the Omnibox to enter a search query and send your search to Google or another search engine.

Entering a Query

You use the Omnibox to enter search queries that are sent to your favorite web search engine. By default, your queries are sent to Google, so it should be a familiar experience.

1. Enter your search query into the Omnibox at the top of the browser window.

2. As you start typing in the Omnibox, Google suggests both queries and web pages you are likely to visit in a drop-down list. Select the query you want from the drop-down list.

3. Alternatively, finish typing your query and then press Enter.

Your search results are displayed in the browser window.

Google Search Page

You can also, of course, do your searching from Google's main search page on the Web (www.google.com). However, you get the exact same results as you do when searching from Chrome's Omnibox.

Understanding Search Results

After you enter your search query, Google searches its index for all the web pages that match your query. Then it displays the results on a search results page.

Interestingly, each results page is unique; what you see depends on what you're searching for. In fact, the same query made on different days, or by different users, might return different results. That's just Google's way of trying to serve the best results for each individual user.

That said, there are some common elements you're likely to encounter as a result of a Google search. These include the following:

- **Ads:** These are paid ads by Google's advertisers. You should not confuse these ads with the "organic" search results because they may have only indirect relevance to your query. These ads typically are positioned to the right of the main search results, and sometimes above the main results.

- **Page title:** For each search result, Google displays the title of the page. The title is a clickable link; click it to view the linked-to page.

- **URL:** This is the full web address of the selected web page. It is *not* a clickable link; you have to click the page title to jump to the page.

- **Page excerpt:** Below the page title is an excerpt from the associated web page. This may be the first few sentences of text on the page, a summary of page contents, or something similar.

- **Local search results:** If Google thinks you're looking for something locally, Google often displays a map at the top of the search results page. Local businesses that match your query are pinpointed on the map, with information about those businesses underneath the map. Click More Places to view even more local results.

Search Tools

You can fine-tune your search results by using Google's search tools. Click the Tools button above the search results to display additional filtering options for your specific search. Depending on the type of search you conducted, you may have the option of filtering results by age (time), type of results (visited pages, reading levels, and so on), physical location, size or color of image, and so forth.

Changing Search Providers

By default, Google Chrome uses Google for all of its browser-based searches. You can, however, change this so that you send all your queries to Yahoo! or Bing, or to another search site of your choice.

1. Click the Customize and Control button and select Settings.

2. When the Settings page appears, go to the Search Engine section and select a provider from the pull-down list: AOL, Ask, Google, Yahoo!, or Bing.

3. To choose from additional search providers, click Manage Search Engines.

4. When the Manage Search Engines page appears, click the Options (three-dot) button for the search engine you want and then select Make Default.

Index

E

J–K

L

Q–R

X–Y–Z

Pearson | livelessons

VIDEO TRAINING FOR THE **IT PROFESSIONAL**

LEARN QUICKLY
Learn a new technology in just hours. Video training can teach more in less time, and material is generally easier to absorb and remember.

WATCH AND LEARN
Instructors demonstrate concepts so you see technology in action.

TEST YOURSELF
Our Complete Video Courses offer self-assessment quizzes throughout.

CONVENIENT
Most videos are streaming with an option to download lessons for offline viewing.

Learn more, browse our store, and watch free, sample lessons at
informit.com/video

Save 50%* off the list price of video courses with discount code **VIDBOB**

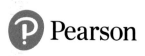

the trusted technology learning source

33164300401168
November 2019